Like the Moon and the Sun

Sanctions Violations of Article 113

Act No. 28 /2014 about Copyright

(1) Any person who with no economic rights infringes referred to in Article 9 paragraph (1) letter i to use commercially shall be punished with imprisonment of 1 (one) year and/or a maximum fine of Rp 100.000.000,00 (one hundred million rupiah).

(2) Any person who with no rights and/or without permission of the Author or Copyright owner infringes the economical right of the creator as referred to in Article 9 paragraph (1) letter c, d, f, and/or h to Use It commercially shall be punished with the imprisonment of 3 (three) years and/ or a fine of Rp 500.000.000,00 (five hundred million rupiah).

(3) Any person who with no rights and/or without permission of the Author or Copyright owner infringes the economical right of the creator as referred to in Article 9 paragraph (1) letter a, b, e, and/or the letter g to use it commercially shall be punished with imprisonment of 4 (four) years and/or a maximum fine of Rp 1.000.000.000,00 (one billion rupiah).

(4) Any person who meets the elements referred to in paragraph (3) which are carried out in the form of piracy, shall be punished with imprisonment of ten (10) years and/or a maximum fine of Rp 4.000.000.000,00 (four billion rupiah).

Like the Moon and the Sun

Indonesia in the Words of an American Diplomat

Thank you for everything Ryan

Stanley Harsha

Stan Harsha
Davenport, Iowa
Sept. 15, 2016

KOMPAS
PENERBIT BUKU

LIKE THE MOON AND THE SUN
Indonesia in the Words of an American Diplomat
Copyright© 2015, Stanley Harsha

Published by Kompas Book Publisher, Jakarta, 2015
PT Kompas Media Nusantara
Jl. Palmerah Selatan 26-28
Jakarta 10270
e-mail: buku@kompas.com

KMN: 40205150076

Cover design: Wiko Haripahargio
Editor: Annisa Genevieve Harsha and Sean Ralph Harsha
All photos in this book belongs to Stanley Harsha unless stated otherwise.

Cover image: Loro Blonyo glass painting by unknown artist in Yogyakarta.
Loro Blonyo is a statue or picture of a Javanese bride and groom, which according to ancient Javanese belief symbolizes prosperity and fertility.

xxiv + 248 hlm.; 14 cm x 21 cm
ISBN: 978-1514817209

Printed by Mardi Yuana, Bogor.
The printer does not assume any responsibility for the content of this book.

TABLE OF CONTENTS

GLOSSARY

apotik hidup: A complete Javanese garden or "living pharmacy".

bakso: meatball soup, a dish President Obama said he loves from his childhood in Jakarta.

bang: brother, also an informal way to address a friend.

banteng: bull

Bapak: Sir or Mr., literally father, a formal way to address a man.

batik: decorated cloth using wax and dye, an ancient Javanese craft, from the word *tik*, meaning to dot.

becak: pedicab

becik: kindness (Javanese)

bendi: horsecart in West Sumatra

blusukan: refers to President Jokowi's impromptu visits to listen to the people's concerns, especially to places politicians do not usually visit such as slums and garbage dumps.

buah-buahan: fruits

budi-unggul: noble character

bulan puasa: Indonesian term meaning fasting month, or Ramadan.

bule: slang word for Caucasian, like *gringo* but with a neutral connotation.

Bundo Kanduang: Earth Goddess in West Sumatra

bunga: flowers

cunguk: spy

datang, duduk, dengar, diam, duit: The five Ds of being shaken down for a bribe by Indonesian officials: come, sit, listen, be quiet, money.

desentralisasi: decentralization of Indonesian government authority to local governments.

empon-empon or *bumbu dapur:* roots used for spices

etika kebijaksanaan: just ethics (Javanese)

gado-gado: Indonesian mixed salad served with peanut sauce

gemuk: fat

gotong royong: community mutual assistance

halal bi-halal ceremony: a Muslim ceremony on the holy day of Idul Fitri to kneel before elders and express love and ask for forgiveness.

Ibu: Mam or Mrs., literally mother, a formal way to address a woman.

Idul Fitri: Muslim holiday following Ramadan with feasting, open houses and gifts for children.

imam: Muslim cleric

jamu: medicinal herbs, facial and skincare potions and flowers used for Javanese spiritual offerings

jodoh: a perfect match determined by fate, such as one that results in marriage or certain mystical matches such as finding the perfect *keris* (sacred dagger).

kain: Indonesian fabric

kaki lima: food pushcarts, literally meaning five legs – the cart's wheel, the cart's two legs and the peddler's two feet.

kamanungsan: humanity (Javanese)

kancil: mousedeer

kembang telon: Javanese spiritual offering of three types of flowers.

kembul dhahar: When the bride and groom feed each other during the wedding ceremony, symbolizing shared happiness and sorrow of the union.

khalwat: close proximity to the opposite sex

Ki Padmosusastro (1841-1926), a Solo, Central Java philosopher and pioneer of modern Javanese grammar and philosophy, who introduced concepts of human rights into Javanese society.

kue pisang: banana cake

kurus: skinny

laku utama: noble, exemplary behavior (Javanese)

"Lapor ayam hilang, kambing pun hilang": report the chicken missing, the goat also disappears, meaning police ask for bribes to investigate crimes.

Lebaran: the Idul Fitri holiday at the end of fasting month.

lemper: sticky rice

lumpia: egg rolls

Mandala: circle of spiritual power

mantep: loyalty (Javanese)

mas: brother, also informal way to address a man

meneng: remain quiet in dignified, discrete fashion. (Javanese)

merantau: to migrate

midodareni: a traditional Javanese ceremony the night before the wedding. The groom visits the bride's family bearing gifts, waiting outside. *Midodareni* is derived from the word *Widodari* meaning goddess, the bride being as beautiful as a goddess.

musyawarah: consensus building

"Narima hing pandhum": a Javanese phrase meaning an ability to deal with anything and survive anything.

nasi goreng: fried rice, a popular Indonesian dish.

nasi liwet: a traditional Solo, Central Java rice dish cooked in coconut milk, chicken broth and spices.

nasi Padang: West Sumatran spicy food

njawani: personification of Javanese behavior (Javanese)

nongkrong: hanging out with someone, literally to squat (Javanese)

ojo dumeh*:* power corrupts (Javanese)

om: uncle, an informal way to address an older man. Equivalent for a woman is *tante.*

pala-gumantung: hanging fruits

pala-kependem: tubers

pala-kesimpar: fruit bearing ground vines such as pumpkin

pantun: Malay oral poetic verse

pasukan siluman*:* "invisible troops" who carried out executions and kidnappings under President Soeharto

pawang: a mystic with specialized powers, such as the ability to delay rain or rid of snakes.

pesantren: Islamic boarding school

Ramadan: Muslim fasting month

Rapai Daboh: An Acehnese dance performed with a dagger

rasa: feelings or intuition

Reformasi: Reformation, referring to the period of democracy, personal freedom, and local political autonomy that began in Indonesia after the 1998 fall of President Suharto's authoritarian regime.

rencong*:* Acehnese dagger

Sabang to Merauke: the two farthest cities spanning Indonesia, 5248 kilometers (3,261 miles) apart. Sabang, Aceh is the westernmost city and Merauke, Papua is the easternmost city.

siraman: a ritual cleansing with sacred water prior to a wedding.

suci trilaksita: one's thoughts, word and actions are the same (Javanese)

suket: grasses

sungkeman: when the bride and groom kneel in front of the parents during the wedding ceremony.

tanaman hias: decorative plants

tanaman obat: medicinal herbs

tanggap sasmita: to read another person's subtle signals

tari Saman: the Acehnese "thousand hands dance"

temen: honesty (Javanese)

teteg: fortitude (Javanese)

tresna-anannga: pure love, for country, family, etc. (Javanese)

walinagari: Democratically elected local leaders in West Sumatra

warung: food stand, with benches, ubiquitous in Indonesia.

wayang: Javanese shadow puppet play

welas asih tanpa pamrih: altruistic love and empathy

ONE PERSON, TWO COUNTRIES: BEYOND PERSONAL REMINISCENTS

AZYUMARDI AZRA*

Readers of Stanley Harsha's very interesting book will feel this work is more than a story about the life of a United States diplomat who was assigned to Indonesia over a period of 12 years. Stanley Harsha spent 28 years coming and going to Indonesia.

Thus, this work is more than the writer's reminiscences. This book imaginatively paints a portrait of society, culture, politics and even a religious journey in the two countries the writer loves, the United States and Indonesia.

Born and raised in Colorado in the U.S., Stanley has a deep love for his country. However, at the same time, his life journey in Indonesia, a half world apart from America, also influenced his worldview, giving him an unbreakable love for Indonesia.

He has passed a lengthy span of time living in and going back and forth from Indonesia--half of his life--as a diplomat, and also as an observer and an Indonesian cultural practitioner. His wife is an Indonesian. Thus, Stanley is in a strong position to compare the United States and Indonesia in a reflective way. Likely, there are not many other writers who can create a work like this.

Furthermore, thanks to his widespread network as a U.S. diplomat with positions at the U.S. Consulate General in Medan and the U.S. Embassy in Jakarta, a "son in law" to Indonesia, Stanley possesses information that is both varied and vast. He has mixed not only in diplomatic circles but also with journalists, intellectuals, religious figures, students, civil society activists, and also, with ordinary people. His ease in speaking Indonesian has opened wide access to talk with everyone in many places in Indonesia.

United States and Indonesia certainly have many contrasts due to differences between the peoples, histories, societies, cultures and politics. However, it is important to emphasize that there are also many commonalities that inspire Stanley to love the two countries equally.

Foremost, Indonesia and the U.S. are equally rich with heterogeneous races and ethnicities, socio-cultural traditions, languages and religions. This variety is recognized in the principle or phrase, *e pluribus unum,* in the United States, and *bhinneka tunggal ika* in Indonesia, both of which mean unity within diversity. The two countries really do represent multi-culturalism in its truest sense.

Another commonality that deserves noting is that the two countries are democracies. Indonesia, since it entered the *Reformasi* era with the 1999 elections, has adopted a system of multi-party, free competitive elections. It is the third largest democracy in the world after India and the U.S. Still, democracy in the U.S. is much more strongly established, while Indonesia is still consolidating its democracy in a process that often appears to be what Stanley, and many people in Indonesia, refer to as "*democrazy*".

Aside from the excesses and unintended consequences from this democratic opening in Indonesia, a Muslim majority country, compatibility between Islam and democracy is clear. Different from many other Muslim majority countries in the Middle East and South Asia, Indonesia demonstrates that democracy and Islam go peacefully hand in hand.

On the other hand, a democratic deficit has occurred over and over again in many Muslim majority countries. Indeed, the democratic openings that took place through the Arab Spring in Tunisia, Egypt, Libya,

Yemen and Syria since 2011, give us almost no hope today. This same tendency also is seen, for example, in Iraq and Pakistan. What has happened in these countries is the rise of violence and military return to power.

Why is Indonesian Islam compatible with democracy? Part of the explanation is explicitly and implicitly presented by Stanley in this book.

To reiterate a point, Islam and democracy in Indonesia primarily have their source in the Indonesian character that differs from Arab Islam or Pakistan Islam, and elsewhere. Indonesian Islam is, by and large, *wasatiyyah* Islam—"middle path Islam", or "justly balanced Islam." With its *wasatiyyah* nature, Indonesian Islam is inclusive, accommodative, tolerant, and lives side by side peacefully with followers of other religions.

With *wasatiyyah* Islam, there is indeed a tendency for intolerance to rise in some parts of Indonesia. However, this trend is more closely tied to the spread of transnational Islamic ideologies and practices, weak rule of law and flaccid political policies by national and local leaders. Throughout its history, Indonesia has never experienced religious bloodshed or war that is massive or long term.

Moreover, with its *wasatiyyah* nature, Indonesian Islam has succeeded in remaining friendly with local cultures and various ethnic groups found in Indonesia. Through a process of indigenization, vernacularization, and contextualization, Indonesian Islam has adapted to and accommodated local culture. The result is that

Indonesian Islam has become embedded within local culture.

One good example is how Stanley experienced his wedding process with Henny, a Javanese Muslim. Fulfilling Javanese Islamic tradition, Stanley stated his pronouncement of Islamic faith. After that, Stanley and Henny followed Javanese Islamic customs, the two traditions coming together peacefully.

Wasatiyah Islam in Indonesia, as presented by Stanley, can and should contribute in a major way to a more accurate understanding about Islam for the United States and the wider Western world. The writer of this prologue fully agrees with this hope, and has spoken about how to develop the Indonesian *wasatiyyah* Islam model to a number of audiences in Europe and America. I am certain, that despite challenges by the generally intolerant transnational Islam, Indonesian *wasatiyyah* Islam is too big to fail. Civil society organizations like NU, Muhammadiyah, and others like these found in every corner of Indonesia, are strong guardians of Indonesian *wasatiyyah* Islam.

Finally, I am certain that readers of this work, Americans, Indonesians and people from other countries will gain a better understanding of Indonesian multi-culturalism, Indonesian *wasatiyyah* Islam and the multi-religious Indonesian community, that are still wrestling with various problems at different levels. However, Indonesia typically almost never surrenders and is always full of hope and prayer for the best for the land that flows through their veins, Indonesia. ✿

* **Prof. Azyumardi Azra, CBE, PhD, MPhil, MA** is professor of history and was previously the Director of Graduate School of Syarif Hidayatullah Islamic State University in Jakarta, Indonesia for two terms (2007-2011, and 2011-2015) as well as the Rector of this university for two terms (1998-2002 and 2002-2006). He also was the Deputy for Social Welfare at the Office of the Vice President of the Republic of Indonesia (2007-2009). He has produced 36 books in Bahasa Indonesia, English and Arabic. He is known as one of the most prominent Indonesian public intellectuals, and was among five Indonesian civil society figures who had a dialogue with President George W. Bush in Bali, October 2003.

PROLOGUE

In February 2014, my wife Henny and I were eating dinner at the home of Mulyawan Karim, the chief editor of Kompas Book Publisher. "Muke" was an old friend I had known when I was press attaché in Jakarta from 2001-2004. He thought Indonesians would enjoy hearing my perspective so he asked me to write this book.

I had recently retired as a United States diplomat and was seeking a new purpose in life. I had spent many years devoted to the two countries I love most, the United States and Indonesia, and was hoping to devote the rest of my life to building bridges across the Pacific Ocean. I had married an Indonesian woman, worked in Indonesia for 12 years as a diplomat in four different postings, and had spent 28 years going back and forth from Indonesia since 1986. I now spend more than half my time in Indonesia.

This book is about my experiences in Indonesia from 1986 up until early 2015, about culture, history, philosophy, and politics, with comparisons to the United States.

The title of the book, *Like the Moon and the Sun*,[1] comes from an Indonesian proverb describing a perfect match. My marriage to a refined Indonesian woman and my devotion to an intricate Indonesian society is like the moon and sun, a yin and yang of two contrasting people and traditions enhancing each other. Indeed, this book has its lighter, romantic side and its darker serious side. Melding American and Indonesian cultures is complicated but the result is exciting, as evidenced by the many Americans who fall in love with Indonesia and the many Indonesians who love America.

In some parts of the book, particularly those that deal with my diplomatic work in Indonesia, I cannot reveal many conversations I had with Indonesians or some of what I learned. The nature of my work was to keep what people told me in confidence. However, much of what I write about can be attributed to public sources. There are many interactions I had with people that I cannot describe in this book. These persons trusted me to keep their secrets. I tried very hard not to embarrass or harm anyone.

This is a book of affection between an American and Indonesia. Where I am critical, it is out of hope for promoting discussion of important issues between the two countries. This book was written for Indonesians but I also tried to make it relevant for non-Indonesians because I want to share my stories about Indonesia with the world. I attempted to use tone and language that both Indonesians and outsiders could enjoy. The English and Indonesian versions of the book are almost identical, except for some Indonesian terms and concepts that I explain only in the English version.

I wrote the book mostly in English. I can read and speak Indonesian fluently but cannot write Indonesian well. My wife, Henny, who loves words and is a voracious reader of both Indonesian and English texts, translated the book into Indonesian. Some terms could not be translated into Indonesian because they are culturally strange for Indonesians whereas using some terms that Indonesians understand would be too vague for English readers. Therefore, in a few cases we chose to convey the same message using different terms. While Indonesian vocabulary and grammar is simpler, for example, than English, Spanish or Chinese, it is infinitely more subtle.

The U.S. Department of State reviewed the draft of this book and made no changes. I would like to thank the State Department for clearing this book for publication in only a few weeks. State Department is very encouraging of its diplomats to publish and of freedom of expression.

I am totally free to express whatever I want but should state the following: The opinions and characterizations in this book are mine, and do not necessarily represent official positions of the United States Government.

The first part of the book is very personal, reflecting on Indonesian and American cultures based on my relationships with family and friends. I write a great deal about Solo, the ancestral hometown of my wife's family and a cultural gem. Indonesian President Joko

("Jokowi") Widodo is from Solo, where I first met him in 2007. The current era of President Jokowi is among the most fascinating, promising and potentially difficult times since I first set foot in Indonesia. I remain hopeful but still guarded regarding human rights and anti-corruption as I follow political developments during the first 100 days of the Jokowi administration. I am hoping for Jokowi the humanitarian visionary.

Part two describes the struggles the U.S. Embassy in Jakarta had after September 11, 2001 in explaining U.S. policy and society. The United States government did not understand the Muslim world at that time and we mostly failed to gain its support for our actions due to this misunderstanding. A culture of Islamophobia grew in the U.S. at that time. On the other hand, interfaith dialogue also increased. I also write about how Indonesia coped with terrorism on its own soil.

Part three compares religious faith and cultural values between the United States and Indonesia. I plead for more tolerance in both countries. I also call for the United States to work harder to include American Muslims fully into American society.

Part four is about democracy and human rights, and Indonesia's amazing success since becoming a democracy. I also am critical of human rights abuses in both the U.S. and Indonesia and argue that accountability for these violations is crucial to both societies. I call on Indonesia to more actively promote itself globally as an example of democracy and religious tolerance.

Part five is about my experiences in four of Indonesia's more fascinating places: Aceh, North Sumatra, West Sumatra and Papua, plus a former part of Indonesia, Timor-Leste.

Acknowledgements

My wife Henny was the inspiration for this book, the translator and cultural consultant. My children, Annisa and Sean, also reviewed the book and helped edit it. In addition, my sister-in-law, Noeke, an expert on Javanese culture, gave me many ideas.

I would like to thank two dear Indonesian friends who gave me helpful suggestions, Djasamen Saragih and IzHarry Agusjaya Moenzir.

PART ONE:

LIFE

"JODOH"

"Salt from the sea, tamarind from the mountain, in the end must meet in the cooking pot." This Indonesian proverb describes the word *jodoh*, which means a perfect match that was fated to be. I had traveled far from the mountains of Colorado to the islands of Indonesia. In that pot of spices I found my *jodoh*.

"Marriage is forever. You must promise to love and take care of my daughter until the end of time," my future father-in-law told me solemnly in the home of my fiancé, Henny Mangoendipoero, in Rawamangun, East Jakarta. I was both moved and intimidated by his request on that March day in 1987. Peering up at portraits of Henny's grandfather and great-grandfather, I made a compact with Henny's parents and ancestors which could never be broken. I believe in karma and fate. The two most important destinies in my life were to come to Indonesia and to meet my wife here.

To the Javanese, a daughter is a gift of life, the one who gives and sustains life. In asking for her hand in marriage, I bonded myself not only to Henny and to the children she would bring into this world but also to a large extended family, closely knit through familial love and tradition. I was committed to adapt myself to this tightly woven culture.

Less than a year before I met Henny, in October 1985, I had just joined the U.S. Foreign Service. I was asked to choose among many countries around the world where I would like to go for my first overseas assignment as a diplomat. I chose the most interesting and exotic country offered, Indonesia, and to my delight the U.S. Department of State agreed to send me there. I felt lucky, as Indonesians say, like I was "hit on the head by a fallen durian."[2]

I was immersed in full-time Bahasa Indonesia language training in Washington, D.C. (The first term I learned was, "*O begitu!*" (Oh really!). After eight months of language training, in August 1986, I landed at Soekarno Hatta Airport in Jakarta.

A couple of weeks after my arrival, I met Henny Mangoendipoero. Henny had just returned from getting her master's degree from the University of Michigan on a Fulbright Scholarship and was at a U.S. Embassy reception for Indonesian Fulbright scholars. Beautiful and charismatic, she was the center of attention. Later, as the party was ending, I was desperate to get her phone number but did not know how to ask. So, as all 20 Fulbrighters were chatting together, I asked all of them for their phone numbers, just so I could get Henny's.

Henny was surprised when I called her the next day. In fact, she thought I was being too pushy and did not want to see me. She finally agreed that I could visit her at her office at the University of Indonesia Rawamangun campus where she worked in the Faculty of Arts and Letters. She was embarrassed when I actually came to her office. When I invited her to eat *nasi Padang*[3] at a nearby *warung* (food stand), she thought, "Does this *bule*[4] (slang for Caucasian) think that I actually want to hang out (*nongkrong*, literally to squat) in a *warung* with him?" She declined.

Still, we saw each other frequently after that, always in the company of both of her sisters. Henny was a little embarrassed to be seen with me since being with a *bule* still carried a stigma for nice Javanese girls. Her father refused to see me for months. *Bapak* (father) would peek at me from the back room of the house and would later ask Henny, "Why does that American keep coming to the house?" However, Henny's family thought I was good for her. They said among themselves, "Henny was not wrong (in liking Stanley). He is like medicine. He calls three times every day."

Bapak relented and met me after several months. A tall, dignified and intellectual man from court society of the central Javanese city of Solo, Pak Padmosawego

Mangoendipoero (known affectionately as Pak Ego or Pak Goong) engaged me in discussions about history, culture and religion. I had a cold the first evening we met so he put clothes pins on all my fingers to cure me with reflexology, forcing me to spend the evening with wooden claws hanging from my paws. No one language could express all of *Bapak's* views, so he switched between his first language, Dutch, to Javanese, Indonesian and English, to find the exact words, leaving me lost in translation. Educated in the Dutch school system in Indonesia, he was cosmopolitan and nationalist. He resented both Dutch colonial rule and Japanese occupation.

Bapak exemplified the Javanese ethos handed down through time from the Majapahit Empire (13ᵗʰ to 16ᵗʰ centuries), that is, *laku utama* (noble behavior). As explained to me by my sister-in-law, a University of Indonesia sociologist, Noeke Mangoendipoero,[5] *laku utama* is defined by nine character traits. Most importantly, Pak Goong practiced *suci trilaksita*, which means that his thoughts, word and actions were always one and the same.

For example, as a senior official with the national railway company, Pak Goong never once took bribes, annoying officials above and below him because he disrupted the flow of extra income. In the Indonesian civil servant system, an honest civil servant could clog up the gravy train and was subject to retribution.[6] When *Bapak* retired, he returned all public property to the government, content to live off his pension and income from keeping the books for other retirees.

Through this behavior, he displayed the *laku utama* traits of honesty (*temen*), fortitude (*teteg*) and loyalty (*mantep*).

Pak Goong was also a national hero, posthumously decorated under President Abdurrahman Wahid for his role in the Indonesian war of independence from the Dutch. He kept his actions a secret his entire life even from his family, so that his family was surprised to hear about his heroic deeds, only learning of his role after he received the decoration soon after his death. As a railway official, Pak Goong played a key role in supplying war materiel by rail to independence fighters. Also, when independence leader Soekarno was escaping from the Dutch on January 2, 1946, *Bapak*, who was Manggarai train station chief in Jakarta, personally guided the train to a location behind the Proklamasi Building in Jakarta in the dark of night. He orchestrated the safe passage of President Soekarno (known affectionately as Bung Karno) and Vice President Mohammad Hatta (nicknamed Bung Hatta) to Yogyakarta, staying with the train until they were safe and avoiding some close calls as the Dutch searched everywhere. The family learned all this only from *Bapak's* friends after the funeral. Soekarno remained in Yogyakarta under the safety of the Indonesian Republican government stronghold.

Through these actions and throughout his life, *Bapak* demonstrated the noble Javanese traits of *meneng* (remain quiet) and *tresna-anangga* (pure love—for country, family, etc.).

March 29, 1957, President Soekarno at Rangkasbitung, West Java accompanied by Padmosawego Mangoendipoero (behind Bung Soekarno, second person to his left, wearing black cap), Henny Mangoendipoero's father.

With family. From left to right: me, Padmosawego Mangoendipoero, Siti Soendari Mangoendipoero, Annisa Harsha, Henny Harsha, and Sean Harsha.

Pak Goong also demonstrated *becik* (kindness) and *welas asih tanpa pamrih* (altruistic love and empathy). His children told me, "*Bapak* never said anything bad about anyone else or had even one argument with our mother." He was a quiet man who led by example.

As Mbak Noeke explained to me, the Javanese have unwritten and unspoken rules of behavior that can only be learned through socialization. Westerners interpret Javanese behavior as simply being polite and avoiding conflict but Javanese behavior is based on a deeper philosophy. No one is wrong or right and Javanese have no right to invade another's space by criticizing them. There are only those who already understand or do not yet understand. Those who do not understand must learn the hard way by suffering the consequences of their actions. Rather than tell someone that they did something wrong the proper approach is to suggest a better way, as in saying, "a better way is like this..."

In other words, the Javanese ethic of politeness and proper form, *njawani* (Javanese personification), is a part of their nature. As one Javanese scholar explained, "In considering Javanese characteristics of *njawani*, these are going to emerge naturally. From their day-to-day actions, there will emerge genuine Javanese aspects that exude politeness and courtesy. Everything that is related to manner of speech, attitude, facial expressions, and actions towards others always represent the Javanese personality."[7]

For example, my wife's mother, *Ibu*[8] Siti Soendari Danoedinoto, also from Solo, exemplified the Javanese traits of *laras* (harmony) and *luruh* (soft spoken). Mbak Noeke told me the story of when a maid stole an expensive watch. *Ibu* discovered the watch hidden in the maid's room but said nothing, allowing her to take it. When the maid left the house with the watch, she did not get far before a woman in the market across the street hypnotized the maid and stole the watch and all of her jewelry and money (hypnotism is a common tactic used to steal one's wealth, love and sanity in Indonesia).[9] *Ibu* said no one had the right to punish the maid because she did not yet understand correct behavior but that she nevertheless had suffered the consequences of her actions.

I knew that *Bapak*, as a father who followed Javanese tradition, wanted his daughters to marry only

With Henny and our children Annisa and Sean, in a garden at Mirasole, Puncak in West Java, 2005.

Indonesian men and not *bule*, so I was nervous when I asked for Henny's hand in marriage. He worshipped Henny's mother and cherished his daughters. So, he was understandably anxious about an American stealing his daughter away. He was afraid that he would lose his daughter to America and never see her again. Before our marriage, he gave me a handwritten list of rules I should follow to keep the marriage happy, in Javanese script. (He translated them for me verbally into both Indonesian and English.) I may not have always kept all the rules, however, the fact that Henny and I have remained married for 27 years is proof that

I have kept my promise to her father, and also that Henny is a very patient woman.

The wedding date was set for August 12, the only propitious date in the Javanese calendar in the foreseeable future. As challenging as it was to win Henny's heart, once the decision to get married was made, the days flew by.

However, there was still another major issue to be addressed—religion. Henny was Muslim and I was Christian. Henny told me she simply could not marry me unless I converted to Islam. I told her that my Christian beliefs are too important for me to convert. We both had strong views on this issue but in typical Javanese fashion, she calmly told me not to worry about this, that everything would work itself out.

She wanted me to meet with a very wise man to learn about Islam. A few days later Henny and I visited Abdurrahman Wahid, "Gus Dur," Chairman of Nahdlatul Ulama (NU), the largest Muslim organization in Indonesia with 40 million members. This future President of Indonesia spent a couple of hours teaching me about Islam at his office. He was so warm and kind that I immediately trusted him.

As he explained how Islam is a religion of love, peace and charity, I realized that there are no conflicts between Islam and my own beliefs. However, I told him I could never abandon the teachings of Jesus. He explained that Isa[10] is one of the prophets accepted by Muslims. Since my transcendental Christian belief did not view Jesus Christ as the Son of God, but simply as a divinely inspired man or prophet,[11] I could accept

With the family at an elephant rehabilitation preserve, Tangkahan, North Sumatra, 2010.

Islam. The more I studied Islamic beliefs and history, the more I came to respect and revere the religion for its moral concepts and contributions to world civilization. I studied Islam in preparation for the marriage and converted.

My family in the United States totally accepted my conversion. My sister had converted from a Protestant belief to Catholicism for her marriage, a very difficult decision. My family knew that I had a worldly viewpoint about religion having studied so many world faiths. While most Americans marry with others of their own faith and race, interfaith and inter-race marriage is also common. In the first decade of this century, 45 percent of American couples were interfaith unions. Furthermore, Americans who married someone of another faith tended to have an improved view of the spouse's faith.[12]

Inter-ethnic marriages, on the other hand, are actually not as common in the U.S., comprising only 10 percent of the population in 2010.[13] However, Henny and I feel quite comfortable together in public in the U.S. Particularly in urban areas where populations are more mixed, such as Denver, Colorado, or Washington, D.C., we hardly attract attention. We are much more likely to attract curiosity in Indonesia, even in Jakarta. In fact, many Indonesians will ask me strange questions when they learn that I have an Indonesian wife, such as, "Did she go with you when you lived in the United States?"

Still, I have to admit that at many social occasions, we find ourselves gravitating towards other mixed couples or at least couples who have lived internationally. We can relate better and exchange stories about inter-cultural experiences. Sometimes when we are with Americans whose cultural experiences are limited to their own community, a typical conversation is like this:

"Where are you from?"

"Well, I am from Colorado and my wife is from Indonesia, but we have lived for the past 27 years in Indonesia, Malaysia, Taiwan, China and Africa," I respond, hoping to be able to tell a few stories about the past three decades of my life.

"Oh really? I have a Chinese friend who owns a restaurant, and she...," the other person says, and then talks for an hour about Asian culture based on their interaction in that Chinese restaurant. Variations on this conversation are Koreans who own a laundry or someone's vacation anywhere outside the United States.

Here is a typical conversation with an Indonesian:

"*Dari mana?*" (Where you from?)

"*Dari Amerika, dan istri saya dari Solo.*" (My wife is from Solo and I am from the United States).

O ya? Istri saya dari Solo dan kita belajar di Ohio State. Anak saya menikah sama orang Amerika dan tinggal di Los Angeles." (Oh yeah? My wife is from Solo and we studied at Ohio State. My daughter is married to an American and lives in Los Angeles.)

And then the conversation turns to the most important matter, food:

"*Kamu suka makanan Solo? Suka apa?*" (Do you like Solo food? What do you like?). This type of conversation is as varied and fascinating as is Indonesian cuisine. ✸

KI PADMOSUSASTRO

After our engagement in March 1987, Henny and I drove together with Henny's brother and sister to visit the Mangoendipoero ancestral home in Solo (formally called Surakarta). Ki Padmosusastro (1841-1926), Henny's great-grandfather, was a pioneer of modern Javanese literature, grammar and philosophy.[14] He is known historically as a free-thinking person dedicated to Javanese literature. He was the first man of letters to popularize Javanese literature in prose, breaking free from the literary court restrictions of Solo. Despite his simple *pesantren* (Islamic boarding school) education, he could read in Javanese and Latin characters by the age of nine. As a teenager, he was already an officer at the Surakarta Court. He also became the editor of the Javanese magazine *Bromartani* and head of the Radya Pustaka Museum in Surakarta. Educated in Javanese tradition, he travelled extensively to Holland and England, bringing back modern ideas of liberating the Javanese from the feudalistic court philosophy.

Ki Padmosusastro

His literary philosophy was to free oneself from poetic Javanese convention[15] (*tembang*), and express oneself in modern, narrative form. Influenced by his time in Holland and by his mentor, the great Solo writer Ranggawarsito, he combined Western ideas with Javanese tradition. His book on Javanese ethics, *Serat Tata Cara,* was an important reference book. He taught people to think freely, using traditional thought to promote human rights. For example, he taught the Javanese concept of *"ojo dumeh"* or "power corrupts." He used the term *kamanungsan* (humanity) to teach about human dignity. The term *"rasa"* (intuition) was used to teach tolerance and *"budi-unggul"* (noble character) dealt with expressing one's views while respecting the views of others. He also advocated for women's emancipation in his book, *Serat Rangsang Tuban,* one of the first Javanese works of fiction written in a modern style. His works were among the first modern non-Palace books in Javanese literature.[16]

Ki Padmosusastro inspired Henny to study Javanese literature at the University of Indonesia, the country's top university. Henny's mother, Ibu Mangoendipoero, had almost finished transliterating Ki Padmosusastro's most important books from Javanese script to Romanized Javanese letters at the time of her death in January 2014, so that his works hopefully can be widely read someday.

Staying in the 19th century Mangoendipoero home in Solo, with its lush garden and steeped in Javanese mysticism, helped me to understand Henny's ties to family and tradition. There was even a ghostly horse drawn carriage that sometimes visited the home late at night, with the click clack of horse's hoofs and voices of the carriage's passengers coming and fading into the night. Faint sounds of gamelan music sometimes were heard at 3 a.m.

Even the garden in Henny's Solo home is a representation of Javanese cosmology, with all the elements required for a healthy and beautiful life: flowers (*bunga*), fruits (*buah buahan*), roots used for spices (*empon-empon* or *bumbu dapur*), medicinal herbs (*tanaman obat*), tubers (*pala-kependem*), fruit bearing ground vines such as pumpkin (*pala-kesimpar*), hanging fruits (*pala-gumantung*), grasses (*suket*), and decorative plants (*tanaman hias*). This type of Javanese garden, once common, is less common in modern day Java. The products from the Javanese garden are essential for health and beauty in Javanese society, providing revitalizing drinks and medicinal herbs (*jamu*), facial and skincare potions and flowers used for Javanese spiritual offerings (*kembang telon*). The complete Javanese garden is called a "living pharmacy" (*apotik hidup*). Years later, when we visited the garden with then Solo Mayor Jokowi, he recognized the importance of preserving such a rare garden.

The Mangoendipoero family has pledged they will never sell the home and that it be used only for social good, not for commercial purposes. The family plans to refurbish the home and make it a center to study Ki Padmosusastro's philosophy and Javanese culture. The great choreographer from Solo, Sardono, at one time used the home's garden to stage free cultural events for Solo's common people, with farmers and peddlers sitting on logs and stones to watch cultural performances. ❀

SOLO

Long considered a stepsister to the more popular Yogyakarta, Solo is now emerging as one Indonesia's great cultural centers, known for its rich dance, music, batik and culinary delights. I often visited Solo between 1986 and 2014, preferring its understated elegance to Yogya's more touristy bustle. We often dined on the sidewalk eating *nasi liwet* (a rice dish cooked in coconut milk, chicken broth and spices), the walkway crowded with rich and poor people sitting side by side.

Solo also has long been a bellwether for political turmoil in Indonesia, a fault line where moderate and conservative Muslim movements meet; a diverse city of ethnic Javanese, Chinese and Arabs; of Muslims, Hindus, Buddhists, Christians and mystics.

The 1980 anti-Chinese riots, the 1998 riots and the post-September 11, 2001, anti-American demonstrations all occurred first in Solo and spread nationwide. After 9/11, Solo unfortunately achieved notoriety as a hornet's nest for radicals and the home base for radical Abu Bakar Ba'asyir's Al Mukmin *pesantren* in Ngruki, located on the outskirts of Solo (although Ba'asyir is not from Solo).

Following the U.S. invasion of Iraq in 2003, the radical vigilante group Surakarta Islamic Youth Front (*Front Pemuda Islam Surakarta, FPIS*) raged through Solo's streets, threatening "sweepings"[17] of all Americans and other Westerners from Solo. They could not find any Americans to expel. I was the U.S. Embassy press attaché at that time, and condemned those actions publicly. Westerners were afraid to visit Solo for several years following 2001, but since I knew and loved Solo, I visited the city with my wife in 2003. Solo appeared to be the same quiet, graceful place I had always known but friends there told us that, in fact, radicals were intimidating the populace and the city was deteriorating. Radicals were extorting local businesses and cultural expression was stymied. I decided that Solo was unstable and not safe for official visits.

Unkempt, unruly and void of tourists, Solo had reached a low point. I was reminded of how the American travel writer Eliza Ruhamah Scidmore, the first female member of the National Geographic Society, described Solo's glory and decline in her 1897 travelogue. She wrote, "At Solo, second city of the island in size, one truly reaches the heart of native Java—the Java of the Javanese—more nearly than anywhere else; but Islam's old empire is there narrowed down to a kraton, one palace enclosure, a mile square, where the present *susuhunan* (ruler of Surakarta), or object of adoration, lives as a restrained pensioner of the Dutch government, the mere shadow of those splendid potentates, his ancestors..."[18]

During my next tour to Indonesia in 2006-2009, I heard that Solo had been totally transformed by a dynamic young mayor who had curbed both corruption and vigilantism. I had to see for myself. In 2007, I made an official visit to Solo, asking to meet Mayor Joko Widodo, who goes by "Jokowi." Jokowi's full story is well known to all Indonesians today but when I first met Jokowi in 2007, I found him to be absolutely amazing, the first truly honest, smart and humanitarian politician I had met during my 20 years of connection with Indonesia.

Jokowi greeted me at his office and gave a brief, businesslike PowerPoint presentation on Solo, its issues, and what his office was doing to improve the city. He was honest about his successes and failures. He obviously knew that marketing Solo as an attractive brand was one element needed to succeed. Then, for the next two days he let me accompany him on his daily rounds, seeing for myself how he conducts his daily *"blusukan"* (meeting his constituents on the streets).[19] He once explained, "Ninety percent of my time I am on the streets. I want to hear the people's problems."[20] He spent his entire days listening to citizens, inspecting progress on city projects and making sure city civil servants were doing their jobs. He delegated everything else to his competent assistants. He quickly fired civil servants who stole money.

The son of a small furniture maker, Jokowi studied forestry at the University of Gadjah Mada. He began his career in the lumber industry deep in the forests of Aceh and then started a company designing and making his own furniture, hiring three employees at first. He grew the company into a factory, and soon was shipping 40 cargo containers to Europe monthly and traveling the world as a trader. He once counted Home Depot and Walmart in the U.S. as his customers.

Soon after becoming mayor in 2005, he formed an interfaith discussion group to open up communications between Muslims and Christians. Jokowi worked with local Muslim leaders and used consensus (*musyawarah*), to convince the radicals that their actions were hurting Solo and to persuade them to leave Solo alone. In less than two years after he became mayor, violent demonstrations in Solo disappeared. Jokowi had changed Solo from a nest of terrorists into an international cultural center, a paradigm of progress and social justice. "I do not want Solo to be defined by terrorists," Jokowi told me.

Jokowi had a simple vision for Solo, one that would open Solo to world trade, investment and culture to benefit its citizens. As Solo became more stable, he convinced international investors and major hotel chains to build in Solo.

Solo Mayor "Jokowi" at the ancestral site of Ki Padmosusastro (the Mangoendipoero home). From left to right: me, Eko Wahyuning Sedjati, Mayor Djoko Widodo, Marsubudi Heru Soeprapto, and Suprapto Darmo Saputro.

He spent a year convincing people who lived along the river, which flooded their homes annually, to move their homes away from the floodplain. He used city government funds to build them nice new homes on government plots, and offered low-interest loans for those who wanted larger homes. I met some people who moved from hovels along the river and had built two story homes out of which they started new businesses.

In 2005, Solo street merchants set up anywhere they wanted, including in front of parks and historic

TERKESAN BATIK : Dubes AS Cameron Hume didampingi Deputy Bidang Politik Stanley Harsha meli- *hat koleksi batik di Museum Batik Danar Hadi di Dalem Wuryaningratan, Solo, Minggu (26/4). (50)*

Dubes AS Terkesan Batik dan Solo

DUBES AS Cameron Hume berada di Solo sejak Jumat (24/4) atas undangan Wali Kota Joko Widodo (Jokowi). Selama tiga hari, dia yang didampingi Deputy Bidang Politik Stanley Harsha mengelilingi Kota Solo, baik siang maupun malam.

Mulai dari tempat wisata Gladag Langen Bogan (Galabo), Pura Mangkunegaran, Museum Batik Danar Hadi, Pasar Gading, Pasar Klithikan Notoharjo, Monumen

Banjarsari, proyek revitalisasi rumah kumuh di Kratonan, proyek sanitasi di Semanggi, rumah relokasi korban banjir di Mojosongo.

Di Solo, Cameron Hume mengaku sangat berkesan. Ia mengatakan, Solo adalah sebuah komunitas yan sangat unik. Meski diterjang budaya modern atau global, namun budaya lokal Solo masih saja tetap terjaga. Bahkan budaya lokal itu terus berkem-

bang. Tentu saja ini membedakan dengan kota-kota lain di Indonesia.

Kesan Dubes terhadap Solo juga menyangkut keamanan kota. Pada malam hari ia berkeliling kota tanpa pengawalan polisi. Menurutnya, Solo sudah kondusif dan itu terbukti dengan banyaknya turis asing yang singgah.

(Bersambung hlm D Kol 1)

Suara Merdeka, April 27, 2009

U.S. Ambassador to Indonesia Cameron Hume (center) accompanied by me as Deputy Political Counselor, with Solo Mayor Djoko Widodo (far right), viewing batik collection at Museum Batik Danar Hadi at Dalem Wuryaningrat, Solo, April 26, 2009.

monuments, the types of eyesores that spoil beauty in cities across the nation. In most cities such as Jakarta, merchants cannot afford to move and oftentimes police simply kick them out, causing the poor merchants to lose their livelihoods.

Jokowi had a more sensible, people-oriented plan. He told me he did a survey of the street market situation and decided on a new approach. He persuaded street merchants to voluntarily move to 38 traditional market centers the city built, housing 16,000 small merchants as of 2009. For example, all the wet market merchants sold their fruits, vegetables and meats in one large market with stainless steel tables and hoses to keep the market fresh and clean. Rent and utilities were free. The hundreds of merchants selling motorcycle parts moved to one organized market, the largest in Indonesia.

As a result, more people went to the wet market to buy food because it was clean and Indonesians across Java flocked to the Solo to buy motorcycle parts because it was convenient. Business revenue for small merchants quadrupled in one year. He also took me to see new community bathroom and kitchen facilities he built with green technology as well as community cultural and children education centers. He provided free medicine to the poor and so forth.

I asked Jokowi how Solo could afford all this, and he said that the City of Solo had plenty of funds provided that the funds are not wasted.

As I walked the city in 2007, talking to people, I learned firsthand that everyone's life was better because of Jokowi. Everyone I met had personally met Jokowi and had stories of how their lives were better. Years later, in 2014, I talked to taxi drivers and street merchants in Jakarta about Jokowi's performance during his two years as Governor of Jakarta. Everyone I met in Jakarta also talked about how free schooling and social services under Jakarta Governor Jokowi had already given them more hope. People's lives were personally touched by Jokowi's leadership. For example, one taxi driver told me he appealed to Jokowi's office to help with medical treatment for a sick child he had adopted, and received Rp.500,000 ($50) for emergency treatment.

Jokowi proudly calls himself a furniture trader but he also is a man of the arts. In 2006, he evaluated Solo's cultural riches, discovering that Solo was home to 440 performing arts workshops – dance, music and theater. Solo also had two vocational arts schools, including the Indonesian Arts Institute Surakarta with majors in traditional arts, including a gamelan orchestra and *wayang* (Javanese puppetry). He turned Solo into a city of international arts festivals.

The second time I visited Jokowi, in October 2008, he was riding atop a horse in a parade at the UNESCO International Heritage Cities Conference, an international cultural festival held in Solo. World mayors chose Solo for this event because of Jokowi's global networking. The rainclouds that morning were dark, threatening to ruin his parade. The streets were lined with 750,000 people, three-quarters of the entire population of Solo. However, not one drop of rain fell on the parade. I was told that Jokowi had hired the very best *pawang* (mystic) to stop the rain from falling on the celebration, one with enough power to stop rain from falling on the entire city. One person said he noticed the rain stopped just a meter above our heads. He told me, "You see, it did not start falling until after the parade." Even a worldly businessman realizes the importance of Javanese mysticism.

In 2009, I suggested to U.S. Ambassador Cameron Hume that he visit Solo to meet Jokowi. He was skeptical because of Solo's previous notoriety but agreed to visit. Jokowi gave Ambassador Hume the same impressive tour. Ambassador Hume was amazed to have found a model of what good governance can achieve in Indonesia and promoted Solo to everyone he met. Thus, in a few short years Jokowi turned Solo from a sad city into what he called "The Spirit of Java," modern yet retaining its history and culture. ✿

Jokowi and Obama

My hope is that Jokowi will indeed represent the characteristics of a Javanese leader in the spirit of noble behavior (*laku utama*), such as the traits my sister-in-law Mbak Noeke writes about: patient, prepared, wise, self-controlled, harmonious, capable, self-actualized, mentally quick, simple, noble, soft spoken and unassuming, with intelligence and reasoning power, watchful and alert, commanding authority and respect, well versed, and superbly competent.[21]

Indonesians are totally fed up with leaders not serving the people, and with greed and corruption. If Jokowi can indeed embody ancient Javanese values of *laku utama*, then he can return just ethics (*etika kebijaksanaan*) to Indonesia.

As I attended the people's party celebrating Jokowi's inauguration as president on October 20, 2014, at Monas national monument, I could feel a calm euphoria among the half million people from all walks of life who attended. Many Indonesians believe he has been blessed with a light of God that will enable him to lead and bring prosperity to the people. Others say expectations for Jokowi are too high.

As I finished writing this book in February 2015, I had no idea which direction Indonesia will go. However, I do believe that the high hopes of the Indonesian people are healthy considering how long their leaders have let them suffer. Certainly, given the chance to succeed, the Indonesian people will succeed.

I spoke to a meatball soup (*bakso*) vendor on inauguration day. He said, "In Indonesia, many people struggle, struggle getting enough to eat. Rich people buy $100,000 cars and many people don't even have a home."

Indonesia's wealthy elite live absurdly opulent lives and Indonesians resent this. When important Indonesians travel abroad and spend thousands of dollars on expensive watches and purses or $10,000 on a prostitute, the word spreads across Indonesia and everyone knows, in Indonesia and in the countries they visit. I hear stories of this type of behavior from friends in Indonesia and the United States all the time. I believe that Jokowi is just as angry at this type of behavior as is my *bakso* vendor friend.

Indonesia Bagian dari Diri Saya

JAKARTA (SINDO)—Presiden Amerika Serikat (AS) Barack Obama kembali menegaskan Indonesia memiliki arti penting dalam perjalanan hidupnya. Bagi Obama, Indonesia adalah bagian dari dirinya yang turut membentuk karakter serta kepribadiannya selama ini.

Obama pernah tinggal di Jakarta dari tahun 1967 hingga 1971. Presiden Afro-Amerika pertama di AS ini mengaku, masa empat tahun meninggalkan kesan mendalam serta turut membentuk kepribadiannya di masa kecil. Lantaran pentingnya Indonesia itulah Obama merasa perlu mengajak Indonesia untuk menjadi lebih baik. Seperti diketahui, lawatan Obama ke Indonesia dilakukan di saat Partai Demokrat kalah dalam pemilu sela (2011).

bersambung ke hal 7

KULIAH UMUM: Presiden Amerika Serikat Barack Obama melambaikan tangan kepada audiens seusai memberikan kuliah umum di Universitas Indonesia (UI), Depok, Jawa Barat, kemarin.

Seputar Indonesia, November 11, 2010

President Obama during November 10, 2010, visit to Indonesia.

Some Indonesians compare Jokowi to President Obama, who also was elected with high expectations to reduce social inequality and lessen the hardship of common people. When Obama was elected, the gap between the rich and the poor in the U.S. was widening. The financial crisis that hit the U.S. hard in 2008, just before Obama took office, revealed corruption and greed among some wealthy financiers in the U.S. and poor corporate governance in some companies. Like Jokowi in Indonesia, Obama portrayed an empathy for middle and lower class Americans. He carried out policies to increase education and job opportunities for most Americans and to provide health care for everyone.

Obama's passage of the Affordable Care Act (ACA) had deep personal significance for me. I grew up living in poverty because of medical bills for my mother's cancer treatment. I witnessed my father suffer a fatal heart attack because he did not have health insurance and had to wait several days to be admitted into a Veteran's Affairs hospital. (He was a World War II veteran.) Thus, I found the ACA to be one of the most important social welfare laws passed in U.S. history. The U.S. is too rich a country to not take care of its ill citizens.

Like most Americans, I also do not want the U.S. to become a social welfare state similar to many European countries. The U.S. is a nation where everyone has to work hard and have skills or education to succeed, and that is what makes America strong. My ancestors were just ordinary people, farmers and small merchants. My grandparents and parents owned a dry cleaners and peddled brushes for a living. I worked my way through school as a cook and as a roofer in order to achieve the education needed to become a diplomat.

Still, the U.S. free enterprise system can lead to excessive greed if not controlled by rule of law. Americans also believe in meritocracy, that even the rich should work hard and have skills to succeed, and not because of family or powerful friends, or because they come from the same social caste, ethnicity or religion of those in power. Americans believe that the wealthy should give back to society. Examples that Americans admire are successful entrepreneurs like Warren Buffett, Bill Gates and Oprah Winfrey, self-made Americans, who gave their wealth back to the world. By comparison, corporate criminals like Bernie Madoff (Wall Street conman) and Jeff Skilling (Enron scandal) damaged the American economy. Many corporate leaders gave themselves multi-million dollar raises while at the same time leading companies into bankruptcy.

Although I could succeed through hard work and education, not everyone in America is healthy and white skinned. The uninsured were only one illness away from poverty before Obama passed the Affordable Care Act. In construction and restaurant jobs, I worked beside some brown-skinned Americans who had difficulty getting better jobs because of their race.

Discrimination is decreasing in the U.S. The fact that Obama was elected president was a milestone in overcoming racism in America. Still, his election revealed a cultural divide. Many of Obama's enemies do not like him because he is liberal. Some do not like him simply because he is black. They have used bigoted lies against him, claiming that he is a Muslim born in Africa who is secretly conspiring to turn the U.S. into a foreign-dominated Muslim country, appealing to xenophobic paranoia held by some conservative Americans. This is despite the fact that Obama has proven he was born in Hawaii and worshipped at Christian churches all his life.

Whether or not Obama is a Muslim should not be an issue. Still, professing Christian values is an important attribute to be elected president of the

U.S. John Kennedy, a Catholic, broke a major religious barrier in 1960, when he was the first non-Protestant to be elected president. Furthermore, Joe Lieberman, a Jew, came very close to being elected vice president as Al Gore's running mate in the 2000 elections, when Gore and Lieberman almost won the election. Many non-Christians have been elected to U.S. Congress, which in 2012 had a Hindu, Buddhist, two Muslims, 33 Jews and a number of members who refused to state their religious affiliation, in addition to many Protestants and Catholics.[22]

Unfortunately, Obama faced opposition in U.S. Congress that was determined to defeat every idea he had simply in order to ensure that Obama would fail as president. However, I believe that history will judge Obama as a determined leader who turned the tide in the U.S. towards a more socially just, fair and tolerant society.

The U.S. is a wealthy land with strong rule of law and an outstanding education system that is accessible to everyone. Furthermore, Americans are hardworking and have a strong family system. The U.S. is constantly renewing its vitality by welcoming the smartest and hardest working immigrants from around the world. The U.S. will remain economically and culturally strong for a long, long time to come, alongside rising powers such as Brazil, China, India and Indonesia. However, power and wealth are not the mark of a great nation. A great nation is also just and kind.

Jokowi also was elected by a slim majority of his people who are hopeful that he can lead Indonesia to be a more fair society with more opportunities for ordinary people. His opponents also made up bigoted and xenophobic lies about him, claiming he was an ethnic Chinese born in Singapore. (There were also rumors that an American political consultant was behind these dirty campaign tactics, which I hope is not true.)

Like Obama, Jokowi is proposing far reaching policy to close the gap between the rich and the poor, including universal health care and free basic education. Jokowi also faces strong opposition in Parliament, and within his own political coalition, by politicians who oppose change. Of course, Jokowi's vision for Indonesia is more far reaching than that of Obama given Indonesia's current state of social and political development, and the obstacles he faces are far greater.

I will close this chapter with the story of another Central Javanese man, Ali Mahmudin, a 23-year-old business management student at University of Airlangga in Surabaya. He is from Purowadi, near Solo. He began his dream to be an entrepreneur at age six, selling cold drinks. To pay for his education, he started with a small wooden box as a store to sell snacks, slowly building the business to distribute to stores products such as soap, cigarettes, kitchen utensils and other small goods. Later, he could afford to buy a motorcycle and build a small warehouse attached to his parents' home. He and his parents now make a livelihood from his small business.

His big inspiration to succeed came from attending seminars where he met inspirational figures such as the economist Sri Mulyani, publisher Dahlan Iskan and Jokowi. "I often listened to them and got a lot inspiration. If you want to be an important person, you have to be around important people," Ali said. Ali represents the new Indonesia. A mental revolution has already taken place in the minds of Indonesia's youth. When Jokowi told the people on inauguration day, "Work, work, and work," Ali already understood what Jokowi meant. ✿

SACRED DAGGER

Whon I first got engaged to Henny, according to Javanese tradition, I had four of the five key possessions signifying that I was ready to be married. The five are: a job, a horse, a house, a *keris* (sacred dagger) and a bird. I had a good job, a car and a house. A bird symbolizes a hobby (I had many) or spiritual contentment and self-actualization, something that can take a lifetime to achieve.

I still needed a *keris*. On our trip to Solo and Yogya in 1987, we spent all of our time looking for a *keris*. Some Indonesians believe the *keris* is a living spirit that finds its own match and that a kindred *keris* cannot be bought. I tried to buy a beautiful *keris* in one shop which the shopkeeper said gave its owner great powers. However, the shopkeeper learned that I would move overseas one day so he refused to sell it to me. It turned out that this *keris* could never cross the ocean and that a Japanese who had taken a similar *keris* overseas had suffered a great tragedy, which the shopkeeper did not want to describe.

Then, on our last day in Central Java, as we were driving from Solo to Yogya, a *keris* summoned me. As we passed an interesting building, I asked Henny what that building was, and she said, "Oh, that is the home and museum of my cousin, Saptohoedojo, an artist. Let's turn back and see if he is home."

Pak Sapto greeted us warmly and gave us a tour of his home and museum filled with his wonderful art. I lamented to Pak Sapto that I could not find a *keris* which touched my soul. He then took me to a case filled with his antique *keris* collection. "Choose one," he said. I could not believe he would give me a *keris* from his private collection. I thought carefully, asking about the characteristics of each. Finally, I chose an ancient *keris* with powers fitting for a diplomat, made by hand in the Solo Court from volcanic metals, with 13 curves, a clear, intricate design (*pamor*) and a hand-painted sheath. *Jodoh*—I was fated to possess that *keris*.

Meanwhile, a committee of dozens of Henny's relatives was planning our wedding, a complex process of three ceremonies, plus a reception for over 1,500 guests. I relished the prospect of marrying such a lovely and interesting woman and all the exotic elements this entailed.

The first ceremony, before the wedding day, was the *siraman*, a ritual cleansing. For this, I needed parents and other relatives to participate, but both my parents had passed away, and my brother and sister could not travel so far for the wedding. So, my supervisors at the U.S. Embassy, Jim and Donna Culpepper, took on the role of my parents and the ceremony took place at their home. Other colleagues from the Embassy, all *bule*, played the roles of brothers and sisters, aunts and uncles.

They took turns pouring sacred water from seven wells (or faucets) over my head, as I sat dressed up to my chest in a fabric called *kain*. When Donna Culpepper took the seventh and final turn and emptied her clay jug, the mentor leading us in the ceremony instructed her to drop and smash the jug on the ground. "Smash it?" she said in disbelief, and had to be told several times before dropping it to the ground. I was cleansed and pure for the wedding. My life as a bachelor lay in shards on the ground as I embarked on a life as a married man. At that moment, soaking wet, I felt purified and ready to start a family. I had no doubt in my mind that I was ready.

That evening the *midodareni*[23] ceremony took place. I visited Henny's home with gifts and then sat outside while the guests all had a great time inside. Henny could see me from behind a partition using a mirror but I could not see her. As I sat there, I also could not believe how quickly our romance had developed. I had first set foot in Indonesia less than a year before and was now committing myself for life

Siraman ceremony at Henny's home, her mother cleansing her with water.

Siraman ceremony at the diplomatic residence of Jim and Donna Culpepper, Donna cleansing me with water.

Stating the wedding vows, witnessed by Hartoro Soewarso, nephew of Padmosawego Mangoendipoero.

to an Indonesian woman and her culture. However, I felt no hesitation and no reservation, only excitement for this adventure of marriage, with all its sweet aromas and new emotions. I was anticipating the next day's sacred vows and the following day's wedding reception extravaganza, where Henny and I would be the center of a grand celebration fitting for a princess and her chosen one. "The Queen and I," I thought.

On the wedding day morning of August 12, I arrived at Henny's home in Rawamangun, Jakarta, wrapped to my bare chest in a Solonese Javanese *batik kain*, with a *keris* dagger tucked behind me. I took an oath before an *imam* (Muslim cleric) and then stood just outside the door to the home, facing Henny. I stepped on a raw egg (inside a Ziploc bag) which Henny symbolically cleaned from my feet. We walked together to the altar and said our marriage vows. The two most touching parts were the *kembul dhahar* when we fed each other, symbolizing family unity, and the *sungkeman*, where we kneeled and pledged our love and devotion to Henny's parents.

Three days later I was wrapped in yards and yards of *batik* and waddled into Balai Kartini reception hall in Jakarta for the reception, to jointly celebrate two weddings–ours and that of her younger sister Saras. Saras had patiently waited to marry her husband, Mas Arya, three days after our wedding, so that, in accordance with Javanese custom, her older sister could marry first. The day was truly like being a central character from *The Arabian Nights*, with a princess, a genie and a flying carpet. As Javanese

Following the wedding reception, Henny and I with father and mother, and with Jim and Donna Culpepper, representing my parents, at the Padmosawego Mangoendipoero family home.

During the wedding reception at Balai Kartini, Jakarta, with father and mother, and Henny's younger sister, Saras, brother-in-law Arya Abieta, sitting to Henny's right.

dancers performed, we began greeting over 1,500 guests and did not stop until that evening.

We spent our honeymoon on the island of the gods, Bali, which was still a rather quiet paradise, where one could feel the Balinese mystique even at the beach town of Sanur. Henny had cleansed herself by drinking *jamu* (medicinal herbs) for months and I remember how her skin was silky smooth and had a natural scent as sweet as jasmine. Her skin is just as soft today.

In the United States weddings are also momentous occasions but seldom on the scale of my Indonesian wedding. They often occur in places of worship or at romantic places – such as on the beach or in a forest. One friend was married deep in the Alaska wilderness where everyone had to hike for hours to attend. The marrying couple often times are free to make personal choices on what kind of ceremony they want, one with hundreds of guests or just a small ceremony with only close friends and family. The daughter's parents usually pay for the wedding and can go into considerable debt doing so. I am saving for my daughter's wedding which I hope will be the most important event in her life. ❀

KEEP IN TOUCH WITH FAMILY AND FRIENDS[24]

From the day of our wedding, I became a son, brother, uncle and cousin to literally thousands of Indonesian relatives and friends who are close enough to call me brother or uncle (*"om, mas, bang"*). The complexity of so many intimate personal relationships was overwhelming for someone accustomed to close relationships with only immediate family and a few friends.

My family quickly bore fruit in the fertile soil of Indonesia. In March 1988, when Henny was seven months into her first pregnancy, we had a *tingkeban* (seven month) ceremony in our home in Medan,

A *Tingkeban* (seven-month of pregnancy ceremony), at our home in Medan, North Sumatra. I has just split open green coconut with a machete, with Henny and mother witnessing.

Holding Annisa during a Sungkeman ceremony, kneeling before father and mother at their home, during Idul Fitri in 1989. Henny is smiling in the background.

presided over by *Pak* Fadhil Lubis, an Islamic scholar at Nahdlatul Ulama University in Medan. My role in the ceremony was to chop open a green coconut with a machete. The coconut milk squirted out the side rather than spouting straight up, indicating that the child was to be a girl.

Annisa Genevieve was born on May 20, 1988, at Pondok Indah Hospital in Jakarta. Dr. Maryunani slept at the hospital waiting for the birth, and she was delivered by only the one doctor and a nurse. I also was amazed when Annisa had a gold earring at age three days, her ears pierced soon after she was born. I was told she did not feel any pain and that this is a common practice in Indonesia.

Three years later, in 1991, our son Sean Ralph was born at George Washington Hospital in Washington, D.C. In Indonesia, we were offered a bed so that Henny's mother or I could stay with Henny for several days while she recovered. The experience in Indonesia was more warm and personal but had there been complications, the hospital in Washington, D.C. was much better equipped to respond. At the moment of Sean's birth, a half dozen doctors and nurses suddenly appeared.

In Indonesia, the placenta and the umbilical cord are of deep significance, considered spirits or siblings of the baby. They must be cared for with great deference. Annisa's were buried in the garden of Henny's parents' home in Jakarta. Sean's placenta was buried in the garden of our home in Virginia.

Of course, in the U.S. we do not consider the afterbirth sacred but we do have our own spiritual and supernatural beliefs regarding children. My mother started reading poetry and philosophy to me from the moment she was pregnant, believing I was listening and could pick up some wisdom at a subconscious level. Although a Christian, she also was convinced that I was reincarnated from a French boy. Later, she was convinced that I was guarded by the spirit of a little Native American boy on a pony that a friend had seen hovering around me.

She also was extremely serious about adhering to European superstitions her German grandmother had taught her. I was never to cross paths with a black cat (bad luck), was forbidden to walk under a ladder (bad luck), was not allowed to step on cracks in the sidewalk ("step on a crack, break your mother's back"), and was horrified when I once broke a mirror, believing that I was condemned to seven years of bad luck. I also was not allowed to open an umbrella in the home (someone would die).

My blood is half Celtic, a superstitious and artistic people who believe in magic and the power of words. We are also outspoken. In my family, arguments are heated but short lived and we quickly kiss and make up. So, we are very open about sharing our feelings with each other. There are very few secrets in my family. Even the darkest secrets are always shared with a brother or sister, and before long everyone in the family knows those secrets.

Javanese also possess strong innate powers of perception. However, feelings are communicated quietly and kept very private. They do not want to open themselves up to others. When offered food and drink at someone's home, no matter how hungry or thirsty the guest is, Javanese tell the host to "not trouble yourself."[25] I am always amazed at what Indonesian children do not know about their parents and what brothers and sisters do not know about their siblings. This is not just a matter of privacy but also a matter of respect for the personal space of others, as I explain later in the section on Javanese customs.

The *wayang* shadow puppet plays which express the system of Javanese ethics is performed behind a screen, and the meaning of the play is cloaked in symbolism. Javanese never get straight to the point so that the Westerner is oftentimes left confused or entirely misses the real point. Javanese use their feelings or intuition (*rasa*) to read subtle signals (*tanggap sasmita*). When unhappy with something or someone, my wife will deliver a subtle sign, a slight twitch of the eyebrows or brushing of my arm to tell me to keep quiet. If someone is rude to her, it suffices for her to straighten her back in a sign for the other person to back off, and another Indonesian will usually understand the rebuke. Javanese begin to read other persons' characters from the first glance, noting body language and tone of voice. Polite behavior demands that Javanese understand subtle signals in responding to others, and lack of intuition can lead to rude responses.

My two children have uncannily inherited this intuition. So, typically in a conversation, everyone in my family understands what was said except me. I require complete sentences to understand. Henny is always telling me that I purposely do not understand what she is saying when I ask her to repeat herself. So, blending my outspoken style with the personality of an Indonesian woman of great sensitivity has required attention to cross-cultural communication. My wife, like many Javanese, can seemingly read minds and sometimes she expects me to read hers. Henny can actually smell my emotions from across the room, for example, whether I am nervous or happy.

My children have always struggled with their own cultural identification, seeking a middle ground between American values of independence and free thinking, and Indonesian values of teamwork and humility. As children in American or international schools, they were graded down for not speaking out enough. As adults, they are appreciated for their ability to get along with everyone and to respect others, in other words, for their cultural sensitivity. They have spent their entire lives deciding if they are American, Indonesian or Third Culture Kids (children who identify with more than one culture). As they got older, they appreciated their Indonesian heritage more and are proud of that culture. They love spending time with their many cousins, sharing so much love and laughter. They greatly miss going out at night to eat fried rice (*nasi goreng*) at push carts (*kaki lima*, literally meaning five legs – the cart's wheel, two legs and the peddler's two feet).

The importance of interpersonal relationships among Indonesians cannot be overstated. Americans also care about friends and family but American circles of important relationships generally are much smaller and we tend to focus more on our immediate family. (Some ethnic groups, however, such as Mexican-Americans, also have extended family obligations). For example, I am committed to regular gatherings with sisters, brothers, aunts, uncles, nieces and nephews, and occasionally with a few cousins.

Many American families will have large family reunions every year or few years but, unlike

A family gathering in Jakarta, 1992.

Indonesians, do not have large reunions constantly throughout the year for birthdays, anniversaries and weddings, attended by all extended family. Indonesians feel a deep commitment with hundreds of distant relatives, all of whom have an important place in the cosmology of Indonesian familial relationships. Of course, Americans also work long hours and do not have maids or drivers, so weekends are busy with tasks and housework. (In Indonesia, it is common for even lower class families to have a maid, providing room and board for someone even less fortunate.)

Henny traces her family tree back hundreds of years, having personal connections with an extended family of hundreds of relatives. When working in Jakarta, I did not have the time and energy to keep up with all of the family obligations. Yet, Indonesians typically wake up at 5 a.m. to begin the daily grind, do not get home until after 8 p.m., take their children to school on Saturday mornings, and still have time for birthdays, weddings, funerals and other family gatherings. There is an expectation to attend events for every distant cousin and friend.

For Indonesians, these are much more than social obligations. These are an essential part of life that they relish. Indonesians are intensely social, talkative and cheerful. If there is song and food, Indonesians are happy. They love spending entire weekends at family gatherings, whereas a typical American family will spend the weekend taking their children to activities or fixing up the house.

Attending birthday parties and weddings for relatives I never met can be exhausting but Ramadan[26] and Idul Fitri,[27] for me, are like the American holidays of Thanksgiving and Christmas rolled into one. Fasting is a ritual that I do find challenging, but spiritually fulfilling. Nothing is more satisfying than breaking fast with family and friends, and the sense of camaraderie and spiritual fulfillment this brings.

Idul Fitri, the most sacred of holidays, is meaningful and spiritual because of all the sacrifice and charity that precedes this holiday. Gathering with family to walk to the mosque on *Idul Fitri* morning, the kids all decked out in new clothes, then back to *Ibu's* (mother's) home for a full day of feasting and socializing, is a day filled with joy. The prayers are followed by a *halal bi-halal* ceremony where we take turns kneeling before our elders to ask for forgiveness and to express our love. This is a sincerely felt expression of affection that holds families together. All of us cry as we ask each other for forgiveness. This day is followed by visiting other homes day after day, a chance once a year to be welcomed into everyone's homes and taste their special delicacies. During *Idul Fitri*, I feel close friendship with dozens of friends.

The extensive love of family and friends also explains how deeply felt partings are in Indonesia, be they temporary or permanent. I am always touched by how Henny's entire family is sad when we leave Jakarta, with hugs, tears and genuine expression of farewell. This also explains why so few Indonesians immigrate abroad – they cannot bear to be away from their family for long!

Indonesians seem to mourn profoundly. Despite all the time and attention people give to their loved ones while they are living, there is still deep guilt for time not spent together, meals not shared and trips not taken.

The many commemorations for the deceased greatly ease the mourning over time. Whereas in America, we are left alone after the first few days following the death of a loved one, feeling emptiness, in Indonesia there are large gatherings of loved ones at seven days, 40 days, 100 days and 1000 days after the death of a loved one. Just as Indonesians celebrate so many life events, they also celebrate the lives of their lost loved ones until the deceased have moved on and the living are healed.

Compared with Indonesia, family units in the U.S. come in many different forms. Increasingly, couples live together for many years before deciding to marry, to make sure they are certain they want to spend their lives together and also to complete their education and start careers before marrying. Young people today take the commitment of love and marriage very seriously. Same sex marriages are increasingly accepted in the U.S. as the natural right of couples who love each other. Some states recognize these marriages so that same sex couples can enjoy the same rights as everyone. Many Americans also continue to reject the concept of same sex marriages. Some Christians believe same sex marriages are a sin while others believe God accepts such unions. This remains a controversial issue, although I believe that over time same sex marriage will be accepted as a natural right in America.

Family is very important in the U.S., just as important as it is in Indonesia. Some family units are extended with several generations living close together. In other families, children are anxious to move away from home as soon as they turn 18 and be independent. This is an important rite of passage, preparing the child to be self-sufficient. Even before age 18, most American children have had jobs, bought cars and learned to be independent. My children grew up overseas so did not have the opportunity to have jobs growing up or even learn how to drive a car. However, they quickly became self-sufficient once they started college in the U.S.

Parents in the U.S. are also much less reliant on their children than are parents in Indonesia, where children usually take good care of their parents until they die. Most parents in the U.S. do not want to be dependent on their children and will do everything possible not to be a "burden" on them. Thus, it is common for the elderly in the U.S. to choose to live alone, even after it is difficult for them to take care of themselves, because they value their independence. This is a matter of pride. The children's decision on whether to take care of elderly parents at home or to put them into a home for the elderly is complicated and difficult for everyone involved. ✸

COURTESY AND HAPPINESS

Smiling and nodding in the U.S. usually means understanding and agreement. In Indonesia, this could mean many things. It could mean I agree and understand, or it could mean:

- I have no idea what you are saying. However, I will do my best to try to guess what you want.

- I understand what you want but I totally disagree and will do this my way.

- You really make me nervous and I am just smiling.

For example, I recently slipped on the stairs and fell down in public in Jakarta. Everyone around smiled at me. I understood that they actually were just smiling to ease my embarrassment although the attention of their smiles made me feel even more embarrassed.

I have had official meetings with persons who do not trust or like the U.S. and probably thought I had bad intentions. Still, they smiled politely, not showing a hint of their real feelings. The world was horrified when Amrozi bin Nurhasyim, the "smiling Bali bomber" smiled throughout his trial. Granted, he was an evil, sick person but some thought he might be smiling to mask his fear and guilt.[28]

In fact, nothing can prepare Americans for how polite the Javanese are. This politeness sometimes results in miscommunication that is very frustrating for Americans to understand. Indonesians are very afraid of being wrong or not knowing the answer. They also will seldom tell someone else they are wrong. My first week in Indonesia, I gave my staff instructions and asked if they understood. They said yes even though they understood nothing I said. I learned that I needed to ask them to explain to me what I had asked them to do.

I am never sure whether some Indonesians will carry out their promises because some people would rather promise me something than disappoint me. I have learned to not be disappointed at broken promises because friendship is more important. Indonesians are very patient and understanding with each other.

Idul Fitri at the parents' home 1988: Photo is in front of a portrait of Ki Padmosusastro, painted by Surono. Back row from left to right: Arya Abieta, Saras Endah Padmiandini, Noeke Ratna Padmiandari, Chocky Padmodariarso, Martati Sih Kamdari, Yarry Padmodariarto. Sitting: Goong Padmosawego Mangoendipoero, Siti Soendari Mangoendipoero, Henny Hendang Padmiastuti, me. Children in front from left to right: Respatyo Padmonarendraputra, Prima Padminarendraputri, Annisa Genevieve Harsha.

This is one aspect where Americans are very different from Indonesians. The worst thing someone can do with Americans is pretend to understand something or to make promises one cannot keep. In fact, if someone promises something it is a matter of great pride to keep the promise. If we ask someone for directions, that person will not give instructions unless the person is certain.

Indonesians will not tell bad things to someone's face but they will gossip to the entire world. In Indonesia, the world truly is a village. Of course, much of the gossip is true. So, secret love affairs are not secrets at all. There are countless guards, maids and drivers who see everything that everyone does.

Indonesians do not curse. When I studied Indonesian language, my instructor told me that Indonesians do not have any swear words. Later, I learned that Indonesians do have quite a number of curse words but they are hardly ever used. You have to be in the company of teenagers to hear much swearing, and mature adults do not swear.

The worst words Indonesians can call someone are not considered all that offensive by Americans, such as the word "dog" (*anjing*). In the U.S., the word dog can have many meanings. Dog can be used affectionately, as in, "Hey dawg! "He is such a dog!" means that someone is a playboy. Someone can be "lazy as a dog." Having "a dog's life," means an easy life. "Dog it," means that one has to work hard to do something. The word "pig" (*babi*) practically has the same meaning in the U.S. as it does in Indonesia but is not quite as defamatory in English.

Are Indonesians really the happiest people in the world? Maybe. A 2013 "Global Happiness Report" by Ipsos said they were, finding that of those surveyed, 92 percent were either very happy or happy, and only eight percent not happy. [29] I asked a very happy Indonesian who was experiencing sickness if this study could really be true. During her long life, she found that Indonesians are very happy.

To prove her point, she told me that in 1974 she visited a poor village in Central Java, Gunungkidul, where drought has kept the people in a permanent state of hunger and poverty. She asked them how they could be so happy. They told her, "If the plant sprouts or if we eat betel nut, we are happy."

Americans also find their happiness from family and friends. My mother was bedridden for many years and found happiness in the friends and family that visited her. She also gave more happiness than she received. As my friend, the television show host Pepeng, told me from his bed where he has been confined for many years, "Life does not end as long as our heart and mind have not died!" ✸

RICE

Eating rice[30] is a must for Indonesians. Growing up in the U.S., eating was an activity squeezed into a hectic life. Usually, I ate as quickly and economically as possible. When times were bad, I ate boiled potatoes. When times were good, meals were sumptuous, such as barbecues with pounds of hamburger, chicken, potato salad and cake consumed in one sitting.

The meaning of food was largely lost to me. In Indonesia, I learned the spiritual value of food. An event in even the poorest of places in Indonesia will offer a package of tasty foods such as sticky rice (*lemper*), egg rolls (*lumpia*) and fried banana cake (*kue pisang*) for everyone. At weddings, a bounty of food for guests is seen as portending a successful marriage.

There are many delicious dishes on every menu in Indonesian restaurants. Even at a sidewalk *warung,* it is amazing how many choices are offered. When I travel, I don't need fast food restaurants, as I am guaranteed to find a Padang restaurant nearby. As Indonesians love to claim, when Neil Armstrong landed on the moon, the first thing he saw was a Padang restaurant!

Rice is at the center of Indonesia's food constellation, a gift from God. Even today, farmers say blessings as they plant rice and when they cut the stalks. The fact that beginning from President Soeharto's New Order (*Orde Baru*) and until today, Indonesia is able to produce a surplus of rice and that famine no longer exists is a very big deal in Indonesia. Rice is a symbol of women and fertility while running short of rice is a curse portending barrenness and poverty. I never saw a host run out of food.

When there is too much food in the U.S., the excess is simply thrown away. In Indonesia, guests will take the excess home in baggies and staff will take food home to their families. If there is still too much food, it is shared with the community in the neighborhood, where people are always in need.

Food manifests itself in two endearing characteristics of Indonesians: Their obsession with food and appearances. Having enough food means being prosperous (*makmur*), which also means being fat (*gemuk*). However, Indonesians are generally are not very *gemuk* and being fat is not a desirable trait in Indonesia. Most people who I have not seen for a while say to me that I have either "gotten fatter" or "gotten skinnier." When I gain just a few pounds, everyone I meet will say "gotten fatter, huh?"

Americans do not like being told that are getting fatter. In fact, this is considered to be politically incorrect in America. I would never tell even my relatives, "Oh, you are fat now!" Indonesians tell me that this is a harmless observation. On the positive side, when I lose weight and an Indonesian comments, "You are thinner," I feel like Ade Rai, the Balinese bodybuilder.

Two aspects about food in Indonesia amaze me. First is the amount of food that my Indonesian friends can eat without getting fat. Unless they are poor, Indonesians eat three large meals a day and snack in between. They eat fried rice, porridge and fruits for breakfast, later a large plate with a variety of foods for lunch and dinner, and fried banana, fried tofu and a variety of other snacks at mid-morning and mid-afternoon. Switching frequently from Indonesian to American food, I can attest the reason Indonesians do not get fat is that basically they eat very few cookies and cakes. Still, with the growing popularity of American fast food in Indonesia, I notice that Indonesians are getting fatter.

Indonesians love durian fruit. The first time I ate durian I thought I would get sick from the smell, even before I tried the first delicious bite. The second time, I loved the taste and the smell of durian—a sweet custard with the slight pungency of onion and the delicacy of a fine cheese. Durian is the most iconic food of the Malay world, a food so unique that it only grows in Southeast Asia. In Medan, once a month my two best buddies and I would get together to eat durian sitting on a bench. We got giddy and drunk on the aroma alone. I introduced a colleague to durian in Medan in 1987, and she took durian into the U.S. Embassy, stinking up the Ambassador's office and shutting down an entire floor of the building. Only in Indonesia can a simple fruit be so famous, complex and unique.

The second amazing aspect in Indonesia is how little food the poor eat and still have the energy to live and work. It is difficult for many families to afford nutritious food, medical care and education for children. As far as I can tell, the only way families can cope is through helping each other out (*gotong royong*), with the hope that at least someone in the family has a little extra to help the entire family survive another day. For poor people, a few vegetables and a small amount of fish are a luxury. Most workers live far below the poverty line and their children are forced to go to work before junior high school. Sometimes, people die rather than see a doctor, or are trafficked (enslaved) into prostitution and hard labor. ❋

PART TWO:

NEW YORK CITY TO BALI

SEPTEMBER 11, 2001

"Planes strike U.S. icons of power," the September 12, 2001, headline of *The Jakarta Post* read. On September 11, just a few weeks after I began my second assignment to Indonesia, Henny and I were watching CNN news in our home near the American Club in Jakarta when we witnessed the nightmarish attacks on the U.S. that would eventually reverberate from New York City to Bali, and from Washington, D.C., to Jakarta. Indonesian and American perceptions of these attacks were polar fields apart. The rubble of the World Trade Center and the Pentagon would reveal schisms between Indonesia and the U.S. that would complicate relations for years to come, but would also lead to genuine soul searching on the meanings of faith, justice and equality.

September 11, 2001, was the worst act of war on U.S. soil since the December 7, 1945, Japanese attack on Pearl Harbor, Hawaii. In New York City, 2,753 people from 115 nationalities were killed, including Eric Hartono, an Indonesian. Muslim- and Arab-Americans felt doubly attacked, first against their country and then by their fellow Americans. Americans felt wounded and shell-shocked. Some Americans blamed the terrorists while others blamed Islam.

Angry and afraid, the percentage of Americans who favored military operations averaged 87 percent, according to Gallup Polls.[31] Americans were nearly unanimous in knowing that Arab terrorists carried out the attacks on New York City, Washington, D.C., and Flight 93, and that Osama bin Laden was the mastermind. Americans were both angry at these indiscriminate attacks and bewildered as to why the Islamic world seemed to hate the U.S. when we were the ones who had been wounded.

Indonesians' reaction to September 11 was divided and this baffled the United States government and the American people. At the U.S. Embassy, we felt like we were attacked twice, once by al-Qaeda and again by Indonesian crowds who screamed at us daily in front of the embassy, calling the U.S. "Satan" and burning the Stars and Stripes.

Personally, I was shocked and angry at this attack on America and very confused as to why so many

Indonesians protested against the U.S. following unprovoked attacks by terrorists. I also was very afraid that my home in Jakarta or my children's school might be attacked by terrorists. The next three years were to be the most difficult years of my life as politics and religion became hopelessly conflicted and confused.

Many Indonesians did not believe that al-Qaeda, Osama bin Laden or Arabs were behind the attack. They rejected evidence provided by the U.S. Government and Western media. A large number of people accepted assertions that the attack was orchestrated by a CIA/Israeli conspiracy to denigrate Muslims and attack Islam. It was difficult for Indonesia's Muslim population to accept that Muslims carried out such a horrendous attack. Even later, after al-Qaeda leaders had confessed to the attack, Indonesians were still uncertain. A 2007 poll found that only 26 percent of Indonesians believed al-Qaeda was responsible, with 17 percent blaming the U.S. government, 3 percent Israel and 43 percent not sure.[32]

President Bush's allusions to the Crusades and an ultimatum to the world to support the U.S.-led war against terrorism reinforced Indonesians' fears that the U.S. military was a threat to them. Bush described the U.S. war on terrorism as, "This crusade, this war on terrorism." In his September 20, 2001, speech, he said, "Americans are asking, 'Why do they hate us'," (referring to al-Qaeda). He added that every nation has to decide "either you are with us or you are with the terrorists." Americans with a knowledge of history shared Indonesians trepidation at Bush's reference to the Crusades, which whether intentional or not, reflected Bush's Christian theological world viewpoint. James Carroll, a U.S. Roman Catholic priest and historian, wrote at that time that he felt vertigo when he heard "the President's use of that word, the outrageous ineptitude of it." He continued, "Religious war is the danger here, and it is a graver one than Americans think."[33]

The U.S. also had historic baggage working against it. Indonesians had not forgotten the role the U.S. Embassy played in providing the names of communists to Indonesian security forces during the September 30, 1965 purge nor U.S. support of the harsh Soeharto regime. An exaggerated belief in the power of the CIA was an urban myth in Indonesia. Indonesians also feared hegemonic power after centuries of being subjugated by the Dutch. U.S. status as the unrivalled superpower in 2001 bred distrust. Even in October 2014, in my conversations with several well educated and influential persons in business and politics, I heard questions posing these same types of suspicions about the U.S. role in change of power in Indonesia, questioning whether the U.S. intervened in the transition from Soekarno to Soeharto, Soeharto to democracy, and Yudhoyono to Jokowi.

U.S. foreign policy also was seen as largely hypocritical. In particular, there was an almost universal belief among Indonesian Muslims that the U.S. supported Israel against Palestine. The U.S. also was seen as supporting dictatorial regimes in Islamic countries such as Egypt and Saudi Arabia, while standing up for human rights only in nations whose governments the U.S. opposed, such as in Libya and Iran, not to mention Iraq and Afghanistan.

So, within weeks after September 11, as the U.S. geared up to invade Afghanistan, extremist organizations galvanized popular unrest to oppose a U.S. attack on a Muslim nation. Hundreds or thousands of demonstrators gathered almost daily in front of the U.S. Embassy. "America is the Terrorist," protest signs read. *Laskar Jihad* (Warriors of Jihad), led by Jafar Umar Thalib, who had fought with the Mujahadeen in Afghanistan, called on all Americans to leave Indonesia and attempted "sweeping" (expulsion) of Americans at several hotels. *Laskar Jihad* found no Americans.

On September 26, 2001, Din Syamsuddin, chair of the influential Council of Ulamas (MUI), an official religious advisory body, condemned the terrorist attacks on the U.S. but called for jihad if the U.S. attacked Afghanistan. This statement, using the politically provocative term jihad, was immediately criticized by some moderate Muslim leaders, including former President Abdurrahman Wahid and Muhammadiyah leader Syafii Maarif. Din Syamsuddin quickly clarified that by "jihad" he meant peaceful actions, fighting in the path of God in a broad sense, not in the form of war.[34] (In the coming years, Din Syamsuddin would be a leader in promoting inter-religious dialogue worldwide.)

Meanwhile, in the U.S., in the wake of September 11, hate crime attacks against Muslims and those who appeared to be Muslim or Arab (such as against

Sikhs or Christian Arabs) reinforced Indonesian perceptions that the U.S. was attacking Muslims. At the U.S. Embassy, we apologized publicly for these hate crimes. We also explained that the FBI took immediate action to investigate and prosecute the perpetrators. Such attacks abated in 2002.

Indonesia was divided over all issues related to September 11, mostly sympathetic to U.S. grief but also totally opposed to war, particularly aggression against a Muslim nation. They questioned whether this war would be only against the Taliban and al-Qaeda or whether the Afghan population would be victimized. These views were propagated by extremists to stir up anti-American hatemongering. However, these sentiments also were deeply held by the vast majority of Indonesians. Reports of civilian casualties, from the very onset of Operation Enduring Freedom, confirmed their fears. Human rights violations and sacrilegious acts against Islam would later exacerbate popular resentment.

Following are some of the headlines that appeared in Jakarta from the time that Bush made it clear the U.S. was going to invade Afghanistan:

"Police Ready to Rescue Foreigners," September 29, 2001, *The Jakarta Post* headline read, quoting Indonesian National Police as saying they had 14 companies of police prepared to protect American assets and escort foreigners to the airport should anti-American sentiment get hotter due to Afghanistan.

"Bush Is in a Blind Rage," October 11, populist *Rakyat Merdeka* reported with a banner headline, above a sensational cartoon depicting a scowling Bush with the top of his head cut off and the skull filled with hand grenades and guns.

The same newspaper on October 5 embellished U.S. military intentions in Afghanistan with the story, "Afghan Is Attacked by Virus," reported by its foreign correspondent, Imam M. Sumarsono, in the "War Field." He claimed in his report that the U.S. had already infected the Afghan people with a "type of Ebola virus."

After the U.S. asked Indonesia and the world to freeze Osama bin Laden's assets, Chair of the Islamic Youth Movement (*Gerakan Pemuda Islam*), M. Said Didu, told the national media, "America is like a sissy, only brave when with a gang, inviting all its friends to kill Osama."[35]

This type of reporting was common in many widely read newspapers across Indonesia for the next three years, emblematic of Indonesian reaction to U.S. post-9/11 actions.

However, U.S. military interventionism was not the only factor at play. Indonesian politicians and the media have always found the U.S. to be a huge, easy target. Outrageous rumors are played up in the Indonesian rumor mill against Indonesian political targets as well. This is one reason why Indonesian politicians had a delicate balancing act in how they responded to 9/11.

President Megawati Soekarnoputri, her ministers and moderate Muslim leaders all condemned the September 11 attacks and expressed their condolences.

These same leaders also called for an end to the "sweeping" of American citizens, which ended by December. In any case, threats against American citizens were not popular among Indonesians, who distinguished between anger against actions by the U.S. government and respect for private American expatriates in Indonesia.

President Megawati was the first leader of a Muslim majority country to visit the U.S. following September 11, visiting on September 27. The U.S. offered Indonesia $530 million in assistance during that visit, an indication of how much the U.S. valued Indonesia as a democratic, moderate Muslim country and regional power. Some Indonesians viewed President Megawati's acceptance of this aid as selling out to the U.S. while many appreciated the support. "Careful! Mega's Been Bought," October 20 *Rakyat Merdeka* reported.

However, President Megawati's government was in a tough situation. Indonesia's fragile democracy had only turned two, the economy was still reeling, and the nation faced secessionist movements and sectarian violence in several parts of the archipelago. Religious-ethnic conflict in the Moluccas the previous year, stoked by *Laskar Jihad* members, had killed over a thousand people.[36]

Islamic hardliners and other critics, for the first time unfettered by the suppression of President Soeharto, were free to vocally criticize the government. Hardliner Muslims opposed a secular, female president while some anti-democratic Golkar cronies of Soeharto vied to restore autocratic power.[37] Even President Megawati's Vice President Hamzah Haz, a Muslim conservative, stated publicly that the September 11 attacks might "cleanse the sins of the U.S."[38] Hardliners wanted to send jihad warriors to fight with the Taliban and called for Indonesia to cut off diplomatic and trade relations with the U.S. Thus, opportunistic politicians and religious zealots joined forces to use anti-U.S. sentiment to stir up civil unrest for their own purposes.

Walking a tightrope, President Megawati's government pledged support for the U.S. war against terrorism, took action to stop attacks against Americans, and stopped Indonesian radicals from sending soldiers to Afghanistan. However, her government drew the line at supporting the war against Afghanistan, which she criticized.

The heads of Indonesia's two largest Muslim organizations, Nahdlatul Ulama (NU) Chairman Hasyim Muzadi, and Muhammadiyah Chairman Syafii Maarif, as well as Minister of Religion Said Agil Munawar, also condemned the attacks on the U.S. and called on Indonesian hardliners to cease calling for a jihad against the U.S., while still condemning the war in Afghanistan.

At the U.S. Embassy, we also were under fire, fending off an angry public while securing ourselves against possible terrorist attacks against Americans. Despite official denial by the Indonesian government that international terrorism and Jemaah Islamiyah were real threats in Indonesia, the U.S. Embassy correctly believed that Americans and Indonesians were targets of homegrown terrorists. We conveyed this fact to the Indonesian government in clear terms. For security reasons, the U.S. Mission reduced its staff by allowing many diplomats and families to return home to the U.S.

The U.S. State Department issued a travel warning urging Americans "to defer nonessential travel to Indonesia," citing that "the U.S. Embassy in Jakarta has received information that indicates extremist elements may be planning to target U.S. interests in Indonesia, particularly U.S. Government facilities, and could also extend to U.S. tourists and tour groups. In addition, social unrest and violence can erupt with little forewarning anywhere in the country. Bombings of religious, political and business targets have occurred throughout the country." A travel warning, first issued in November 2000, almost a year before the September 11 attacks and reissued regularly after September 11, 2001, would remain in effect until May 2008, with only slight changes in wording over time about the nature of the threat.[39] This bothered the Indonesian government because of the warning's damage to Indonesia's image and its ability to attract tourists and foreign investors.

Protests in front of the U.S. Embassy and Consulates grew, at times to over 10,000 demonstrators, with rock throwing, American flag burning and attempts to enter the Embassy compound. Some days we were trapped inside the Embassy until nighttime by masses of protesters. This was frightening for Americans and even more so for local Indonesian employees, who worked alongside us throughout the ordeal. Indonesian employees also were subject to personal criticism from their acquaintances because they worked for the U.S. The Embassy put up steel plates to cover windows of one building facing the street. Barbed wire barriers outside the Embassy walls made the Embassy appear like a fortress, a point of contention with the Governor of Jakarta.

By October, the U.S. was bombing and invading Afghanistan. On October 21, a *Tempo Magazine* survey found that 89 percent of Indonesians opposed the bombing campaign in Afghanistan.

Ambassador Robert Gelbard, whose direct style had worked successfully as special envoy for the Balkans prior to being appointed to Indonesia, ran into a juggernaut of Indonesian nationalism during his final months in Indonesia. His frank messages to convince the Indonesian government on the urgency of confronting terrorist threats and protecting Americans from extremist threats were met with strong reactions defending Indonesian pride and dignity. Gelbard complained about the security of U.S. citizens to Susilo Bambang Yudhoyono, Coordinating Minister for Political, Law and Security Affairs, who responded that the government was increasing security but could not stop people from protesting.[40]

Gelbard told the Indonesian Parliament (DPR) that Indonesia risked losing foreign investment if it did not increase security. In reaction, Mr. Permadi (like many Indonesians, he has only one name), a member of Parliament famous for his psychic abilities, quoted the words of former President Soekarno, who once told the U.S. to "go to hell with your aid." According to media reports, Permadi told Gelbard, "I said we don't need them (the U.S.). I even said, if there is no equality (between the U.S. and Indonesia) and (the U.S.) regards itself as the boss and we its slaves, then I said go to hell... We want our nation to be respected."[41] ❁

CALMING AN
ANGRY PUBLIC

In the face of this opposition, the U.S. Embassy embarked on an aggressive public diplomacy campaign, under the leadership of one of America's most empathetic and hardworking diplomats, Greta Morris, Counselor for Public Affairs. As head of the Information Section, I directed the information campaign, although the efforts I describe below were a large team effort.

The U.S. Embassy sent out a barrage of fact sheets daily promoting U.S. policy to hundreds of media and influential people. We arranged for dozens of interviews with U.S. scholars and religious leaders. Most importantly, we reached out to Indonesian leaders to gain their support in condemning terrorism and explaining that Islam is a religion of peace. For example, in December, we distributed a half million copies of an authoritative State Department booklet, "The Network of Terrorism," translated into Indonesian, which laid out the facts of al-Qaeda's links to terrorism, distributing it to over 3,000 *pesantren* (Islamic boarding schools) and other Islamic institutions.

Ambassador Ralph "Skip" Boyce arrived in October 2001, creating a calm atmosphere in the Embassy. During a stressful time when Indonesian animosity towards U.S. policy was boiling over, Ambassador Boyce conveyed clear, honest messages without offending Indonesians. His sense of humor disarmed hostile audiences. On his arrival in Jakarta, the newspaper *Koran Tempo* ran a story on Boyce that typified the attitude he brought, headlined, "Boyce and Jakarta Sympathy, can he bring a friendly attitude that will attract Indonesian Muslim sympathy?"

Boyce used empathy to soften angry critics of U.S. foreign policy. Very soon after he arrived in Jakarta, Boyce attended a long discussion with representatives from 38 Muslim organizations, including from the extremist Islamic Defenders Front (*Front Pembela Islam, FPI*), in an event organized by Muhammadiyah Chair Din Syamsuddin. Ambassador Boyce spoke very little but rather listened to each representative and promised to report their views to Washington. The atmosphere was friendly. At another time, when

U.S. Ambassador to Indonesia Ralph L. Boyce with Chairman of Nahdlatul Ulama, K.H. Hasyim Muzadi during a dialogue before pesantren university students at Al-Hikam pesantren in Malang, November 10, 2003.

demonstrators from the conservative Islamic political party, Prosperous Justice Party (PKS), rallied in front of the U.S. Embassy, Ambassador Boyce sent me to the front gate to invite the demonstration leaders into the embassy for a friendly chat. Afterwards, the leaders told the demonstrators, "Everybody can go home now. We met with the Ambassador and he will convey our message to Washington." The important element he brought to U.S. diplomacy in Jakarta was a willingness to listen more than lecture.

The key public affairs messages we delivered to the Indonesian public were:

1. The September 11 attacks were against the entire democratic world which should unite in this battle. The war against terrorism is against terrorists, not Muslims.

2. The war in Afghanistan was to free the Afghan people from the Taliban who protected al-Qaeda.

3. The U.S. and its people respect Islam and protect Muslims from discrimination.

4. U.S. supports the Afghanistan people with assistance and has a goal of rebuilding Afghanistan.

5. U.S. respects Indonesia and wants to work as a partner in the war against terrorism. Terrorism is also a real threat in Indonesia.

In retrospect, I realize that we mostly failed on the first two points, had some success in convincing Indonesians that the U.S. respects Islam, and succeeded in the message that we supported the Afghan people. We had mixed results on the message of achieving cooperation with Indonesia in fighting terrorism at first, that is until the October 2002 Bali bombing changed reality for Indonesians and they understood that terrorism also threatened them directly. Later, our public diplomacy campaign to defend the war in Iraq would prove even more difficult than the campaign regarding Afghanistan.

At the very least, we convinced even the most skeptical media to print and broadcast the U.S. side on all these issues.

U.S. Ambassador to Indonesia Ralph L. Boyce presenting gifts to orphans at the Hairun Nisaa home in South Jakarta, November 13, 2003.

Given the extreme Indonesian skepticism of the U.S. war against terrorism and in Afghanistan, I engaged in personal diplomacy with the Indonesian media in order to have deeper discussions of the issues. I interacted regularly with publications such as *Koran Tempo, Kompas and Media Indonesia* and also interacted almost daily with publications that reached important Muslim and nationalist audiences, such as *Sabili, Republika, Pelita,* and *Rakyat Merdeka.*

All the national newspapers faced threats from radical groups when they published positive articles about the U.S. or even views supporting religious tolerance. Editors said they received threats of violence against staff and themselves because they published such material. Religious extremists sometimes raided news offices, beat up journalists and demanded "fines" in response to some articles, such as editorials by moderate Muslim scholars.[42]

In November 2001, I visited an Islamic magazine with anti-American and anti-Jewish views, *Sabili*, with over a half million readers. I expected a cold reception. However, I liked the chief editor, Ubay Salman, and we became immediate close friends. We had reasonable discussions and he listened carefully to what I said about the U.S., religion, Judaism and so forth.

Sabili continued to publish hateful articles but at least the editors understood my views, printed U.S. rebuttals and came to dislike the more extreme articles that *Sabili* published. The chief editor and a reporter went to the U.S. on State Department journalism tours to learn about religion in the U.S. and wrote many fair, insightful articles. In turn, I learned about the real life concerns of devout, conservative Muslims through my friendship with Ubay.

Pelita newspaper, a secular and moderate Muslim-oriented newspaper, was helpful in promoting tolerant messages. Chief Editor Rusli Haudy was concerned about Islamic extremism and gave sound advice on how to reach the Muslim public with messages of moderation. He helped us to provide copies of a five-set book about U.S. history, literature, government, economics and geography to more than a thousand *pesantren* in Indonesia. In all, we distributed 100,000 copies of the books. Five years later, I learned that the books were still on the shelves of many *pesantren*, worn out but still read. As *Pelita* editors explained to me, only a few *pesantren* were led by radical *kiai* (headmasters). The rest were led by open-minded *kiai*. The vast majority of *pesantren* simply lacked learning materials of any kind. To moderate the thinking of the more extreme *pesantren*, we needed to provide knowledge.

I also focused on *Republika* daily newspaper, founded by the Association of Indonesian Muslim Scholars (*Ikatan Cendekiawan Muslim Indonesia, ICMI*) in 1993, the most influential newspaper for mainstream Muslims in Indonesia. Its readers ranged from moderate to conservative Muslims. A secular newspaper with a Muslim slant, its staff also included moderate to conservative thinkers, and it endeavored to present balanced news. However, from the U.S. Embassy viewpoint, *Republika* seemingly printed only negative news about U.S. foreign policy, particularly regarding the war against terrorism and policy in the Middle East and Afghanistan.

I visited *Republika* often and had conversations over meals with some of its key staff. They were willing to listen to my views about *Republika* news coverage of the U.S. and occasionally print our official press releases on issues. They also gave me a deeper understanding of the mainstream Muslim readership's views. Overall, however, *Republika's* editors were unconvinced that Muslim terrorists carried out the 9/11 attacks. They believed that the wars against terrorism, and in Afghanistan and Iraq, targeted Islam and Islamic countries, including Indonesia.[43]

Our main messages fell on deaf ears in the mainstream Muslim media:

On the point that Osama bin Laden and not CIA or Israel carried out the September 11 attacks and that Taliban and bin Laden were a threat to world peace, the media were skeptical, even after we presented strong evidence. Most stories asserted that CIA/Israel carried out the attack. Using obscure sources, *Republika* published articles such as one headlined, "4,000 Jewish workers on holiday when WTC destroyed, Israel knew attack plan." Ironically, the fact that all those accused of carrying out the attacks were Arabs and Muslims reinforced the view of many Indonesian Muslims that the U.S. or Israel framed Muslims to denigrate and attack Islam.

We also failed in the message that the September 11 terrorist attack was not an attack against the U.S. but an attack against the democratic world. Instead, most media coverage conveyed the message that terrorism emerged as a result of unjust U.S. foreign policy, which was perceived as holding double standards, particularly with regard to the Israel-Palestine conflict.

The U.S. furthermore failed on another key message that the war against terrorism was not against Islam. Coverage in Muslim press instead emphasized stories that supported the view that the U.S. war was against Islam and Muslims. Islamic media focused on Bush's terms "crusade" and "Operation Infinite Justice," as further indications of U.S. intentions to attack Islam. They also published many articles about discrimination and physical attacks against Muslims in the West as well as about civilian victims of the campaign in Afghanistan. In my conversations with even the moderate editors at *Republika,* they questioned the real U.S. motive in Afghanistan as perhaps imperialistic, allegedly to control Middle East and South Asian oil fields.

Furthermore, the rumor that the U.S. also planned to invade Indonesia was widespread in Indonesia. Populist newspaper *Rakyat Merdeka* in a September 26, 2001, headline warned, "Crazy! U.S. War Ship Will Pass by Indonesia: U.S. also will invade Indonesia, Malaysia, the Philippines."

Claims that the U.S. was behind all terrorist attacks in order to attack Islam and Indonesia would be a common allegation following every major terrorist attack that occurred in Indonesia in the coming years. A 2006 Pew survey revealed that four out of five Indonesians were "somewhat or very worried" that the U.S. might invade Indonesia.[44]

One notable success my office had in the Muslim-oriented media was in conveying our compassion for the Afghan and Indonesian peoples through humanitarian assistance, and, to a mixed degree, support for the war against terrorist threats in Indonesia. Indonesians at least could agree that U.S. policy to provide humanitarian aid and education is positive.

Important newspapers also printed articles criticizing actions against Americans, such as calls for "sweeping" Americans and to cut off trade and diplomatic relations, reflecting Indonesian government and general public views. In my conversations with *Republika's* Deputy Chief Editor Mustafa Kamil, he disagreed with the hardliners threatening Americans. He realized that such actions would only hurt Indonesia, which welcomed U.S. tourists and investment. After one discussion I had with Mustafa, in which I emphasized how dangerous these threats were to Americans, he wrote an editorial calling for an end to these threats.

By December 2001, cooler heads had begun to prevail in Indonesia. As a leading political thinker Jusuf Wanandi wrote at that time, "The views of mainstream Muslims are that terrorism, as propagated by Osama bin Laden and al-Qaeda, cannot be condoned by Muslims. The calls for 'sweeping' against Americans and the campaign for breaking relations with the U.S. are against Indonesian national interest."[45] ✸

BALI BOMBING

Even as Indonesian terrorists were hatching plans for horrific terrorist attacks inside Indonesia, the Indonesian government was mostly in a state of denial, finding it hard to accept or admit that Indonesia faced a domestic terror threat. The first official acknowledgment that there might be terrorists in Indonesia came in December 2001 from National Intelligence Agency (BIN) Chief Abdullah M. Hendropriyono, who made a public statement acknowledging that al-Qaeda was operating in Indonesia,[46] although it would take another 10 months before Indonesia would be forced by the Bali bombing to fully accept the harsh reality of Indonesian terrorism.

By January 2002, emotions regarding the war against terrorism and in Afghanistan subsided. News coverage focused less on these issues and protests were fewer. The U.S. Embassy returned to the business of pursuing the full range of bilateral diplomatic issues while still pursuing cooperation in counterterrorism.

However, as civilian casualties in Afghanistan mounted, my office struggled with that issue. We tried explaining to the media about efforts made to avoid civilian casualties and expressing our regret for collateral damage. These excuses were given little play in the Indonesian media and did not convince many people.

On January 7, 2002, Deputy Secretary of Defense Paul Wolfowitz told *The New York Times* about U.S. interest in eliminating terrorist safe havens in several countries, including Indonesia. He noted the will by the Indonesian government to fight terrorism but expressed concern that "the Indonesian government is extremely weak in parts of Sulawesi and the Moluccas."[47] The *Jakarta Post* ran a headline following publication of that interview reassuring the public that "Wolfowitz rules out direct U.S. attack on Indonesia," which typified how worried many Indonesians were that the war against terrorism might lead to an attack against Indonesia.

In June 2002, U.S. Assistant Secretary of State for East Asian and Pacific Affairs James Kelly told *The Australian* newspaper that Indonesia is a country where terrorists might launch the next attacks, adding that the denial of this possibility by a number of Indonesian politicians made it more difficult for Indonesia to deal with terrorism.

Secretary of State Colin Powell's August 2002 visit to Indonesia helped improve relations, focusing in part on counterterrorism. Indonesian Foreign Minister Hassan

Wirajuda told the media after meeting with Powell, "Indonesia should strengthen its capability to counter terrorism both at home and along its border areas....We have been working with the U.S. toward that end." Indonesia was beginning to publicly acknowledge the threat.[48]

Then, on September 10, 2002, the U.S. Embassy closed briefly due to credible and specific terrorist threats, although no one knew when or where an attack might occur. By late September, Indonesia began to arrest suspected terrorists such as Omar al-Faruq. Abu Bakar Ba'asyir, the spiritual leader of the Indonesia-based terrorist group *Jemaah Islamiyah* (JI), became a person of interest.[49]

Stories began to circulate that all this was a sinister plot by the U.S. *Rakyat Merdeka* reported on September 22, "It is known, America wants to kill Megawati. Scenario: 1. Disseminate false news about the matter of murdering Mega. 2. Nationalists (Mega) and Islam will kill each other. 3. Without needing to use its own hand, American destroys Abu Bakar Ba'asyir's friends, Indonesia Tense." Such stories were so outlandish that it was impossible to even understand the logic, let alone respond.

However, the storyline was about to change.

On Saturday, October 12, at 11:05 p.m. terrorists set off a bomb in Kuta, Bali, killing 202 people, including 88 Australians, 38 Indonesians, 27 Britons and 7 Americans. This was Indonesia's September 11, and for my family, it felt just as devastating. By Monday morning, the U.S. Embassy ordered non-essential staff and all family members to evacuate to the United States. My wife and two children departed by Friday, while I stayed behind.

My family had never been separated from me so we went through a great deal of pain until next May when my family rejoined me. This evacuation was very traumatic for my family. My children had to leave their school in the middle of the school year and resettle in Washington, D.C. They were worried about my safety the entire time they were in the U.S.

At the U.S. Embassy, we were inundated with public and media queries about the bombing, and gave non-stop interviews. This would continue unabated for months. From 6 a.m. until midnight every day I fielded media queries, gave interviews and arranged for interviews with Ambassador Boyce and other Embassy officials.

Right after the Bali bombing, the U.S. was again accused of a grand conspiracy to undermine Islam. Radicals led by Abu Bakar Ba'asyir disseminated disinformation immediately after the bombing that the U.S. Government was behind it. On October 14, Ba'asyir held a press conference where he claimed that America did not lose any lives (*untrue*)[50] and the U.S. had the most to gain from the attacks as an excuse to destroy political Islam in Indonesia. Ba'asyir added, "That bomb was very sophisticated. How could a Muslim person possibly do that?"[51]

This disinformation spread so immediately that it was obvious to me that this black propaganda campaign had been planned before the bombing to shift blame. This story spread by radicals claimed that the bomb contained C4 explosive material (*it did not contain C4*) which only the U.S. manufactures (*also false*). Later a theory emerged alleging that the bomb was so powerful that is was actually a "micro nuclear bomb" that the U.S. had secretly developed (*a bizarre story*).[52]

To our shock and dismay, this type of story was carried as news in both conservative Islamic media and in more moderate mainstream media. These rumors persisted for a long time after the attack and to this day are believed by some. We refuted these lies repeatedly. Ambassador Boyce gave media interview after interview laying out the facts. Paul Wolfowitz told Jakarta's SCTV television that the allegation was an "unbelievable fantasy."[53] *Jakarta Post* Chief Editor Endy M. Bayuni questioned at one conference why Indonesian newspapers consistently carried such false and damaging rumors that contributed nothing to public understanding of the real threat.

So, while the media were focusing on myths, the real terrorists were gloating over their success in framing the U.S. for their heinous murders.

However, the Indonesian government's efforts to combat terrorism had reached the tipping point, with dizzying speed. "Ba'asyir taken to Jakarta for questioning," October 29, *Jakarta Post* reported. "RI Issues Regulations to Fight Terrorism," the *Jakarta Post* reported on October 19, when President Megawati signed tough legislation that would empower the Indonesian government to crack down on hundreds of terrorists in the next few years. "Bali Suspect Confesses to Bombing," the November 8 headline read. "Amrozi Names Samudra a Mastermind of Bali Blast," the *Jakarta Post* reported on November 14.

Indonesian law enforcement surprised everyone with how quickly they arrested suspects with a number of arrests in November 2002. Eventually the perpetrators would all serve long prison sentences or be sentenced to death. Arrests or killing of terrorists by police would snowball in the coming years. As Deputy Political Counselor at the U.S. Embassy Jakarta from 2007-2009, I observed firsthand that, despite a slow start, achievements by the Indonesian government in eradicating terrorism and radicalism have been a tour de force. Many heroic police were targets of terrorists and some died in the fight. I owe my life and that of fellow Americans to Indonesian police.

Still, arrests of terrorist suspects were also controversial. The October 29, 2002, Islamic-oriented *Republika* headline read, "Ba'asyir taken by force to Jakarta." In most newspapers, photos of *Majelis Mujahidin Indonesia* (MMI) leader Abu Bakar Ba'asyir after his arrest depicted a very sympathetic figure, in some photos a smiling avuncular old man and at other times defiantly raising his index finger as if pointing out his innocence. He sometimes looked tired and defeated, especially on court dates—pictured in a hospital bed breathing through oxygen tubes, the image of a dying grandfather.

Meanwhile, influential Muslim leaders raised questions about whether terrorist suspects arrested for being linked to the Bali bombing were victims of Islamophobia and U.S. policy. President of the Prosperous Justice Party (PKS) Hidayat Nur Wahid said on October 14, "We reject the negative image against Muslims that is always connected to events like the bomb explosion in Bali."[54]

After Ba'asyir was arrested, Syafii Maarif, Chairman of Muhammadiyah, Indonesia's second largest Muslim organization with 30 million members, warned against the

Indonesian government widening its net to more Islamic leaders. He said, "Don't let that happen; if it happens we are going to cry out...I am certain that Ba'asyir has merely been made a victim to fulfill the request of a country that likes to dictate—who else if not the U.S."[55]

Ordinary Indonesians responded to the Bali bombing with courage and dignity. I attended an international film festival soon after the Bali bombing in downtown Jakarta with everyone still in shock. The turnout was good despite the atmosphere of trepidation. The organizer announced that the film festival would go on and that we should all demonstrate to the terrorists that their actions will not change our lives. I thought how calm and resilient Indonesians are, able to cope with almost any adversity and get on with their lives. Indonesians have lived constantly with earthquakes, volcanic eruptions, tsunamis, flooding, mudslides, poverty, cruelty and violence. Throughout it all, Indonesians have been survivors, drawing on their stoic sense of faith, family and community for comfort. As my sister-in-law Mbak Ness explained, *Narima hing pandhum* is a Javanese phrase meaning an ability to deal with anything and survive anything, which is woven into the Indonesian culture.

I traveled to Bali frequently after the bombing. I stayed in five-star hotels which had been packed just a few months before at $200 a night. I was sometimes one of just a few guests, paying less than $50 a night for a plush room. The Balinese were brave and resilient. Hotels and restaurants all tried to keep on all staff on reduced wages despite having practically no tourists for over a year after October 12, 2002. Bali was to experience yet another attack in 2004 and bounce back yet again. Still, within a few years, Bali was again thronging with tourists.

By spring 2003, the U.S. was gearing up to attack Iraq, yet another Muslim nation. This war was even more difficult for the Indonesian people to accept. We worked to make the case against Saddam Hussein as an evil leader who threatened the world with weapons of mass destruction.

Still, the media and public were very negative about this war. The media called President Bush "cowboy Bush." A 2006 Pew survey revealed that 54 percent of Indonesians thought the war in Iraq made the world a less safe place.[56] Indonesians had no patience for this war so the U.S. Embassy had to be delicate in how strongly we defended it.

In response to the Iraq war, the Indonesian government made every effort to promote calm. Coordinating Minister for People's Welfare Jusuf Kalla held a meeting on March 19 with Muslim civil society leaders, stating that the impending war was not against Islam nor the Iraqi people.

In a December 10 meeting with Ambassador Boyce, Foreign Minister Hassan Wirajuda (educated at three of the United States' top universities: Harvard, Tufts and University of Virginia) noted that "...the U.S. invasion of Iraq constituted a radical new matter in the U.S. Since the September 11 attacks, U.S. policy seemingly has applied 'the American way' for international problems, that is a one-sided way or unilateral that is based on military power. America needs to return to its original policy."[57]

JW MARRIOTT
JAKARTA BOMBING

At lunchtime on August 5, 2003, we were shocked yet again by a car bomb at the JW Marriott and Ritz-Carlton hotels at Mega Kuningan, Jakarta, killing 12 and injuring 150, including diners in the Marriott coffee shop. I was at my desk at the U.S. Embassy at the time and got a phone call just 10 minutes after the explosion from a journalist friend who was in the hotel at the time of the bombing.

As an indication of how quickly false rumors or perhaps black propaganda spread by terrorists works, this journalist told me that the story already circulating around the hotel was that the U.S. Embassy had advance notice of the bombing and had moved Americans out of the hotel. Searching the Internet, I found that the Indonesian Internet news service Detik.com already had an article with this same disinformation. I had to work quickly to contact all Indonesian media to inform them that this was a false rumor.

Within days of this bombing, Indonesian police had identified suspects and many arrests came quickly. Some of the terrorists would take years to locate and arrest.

One American friend, a family man who had contributed greatly to Indonesia's economic development through business, was badly injured by the blast. The JW Marriott was a favorite meeting place for Americans. I was close friends with the American manager and many staff, working together with them to build homes for the poor in Habitat for Humanity projects. The JW Marriott and its Indonesian staff also handled the attack with humanity and bravery. The hotel was renovated and reopened with stronger security within five weeks of the bombing, and the victims and their families were given long-term treatment and support.

By the time of the Marriott bombing, the U.S. Embassy had learned how to cope with terrorist threats without too much disruption to diplomats' lives. Even though the bombing took place in Jakarta not far from our workplace and homes, no one was evacuated and our lives continued normally.

I realized how much progress the U.S. and Indonesia had made in finding a common understanding of the terrorist threat when I read the newspaper *Republika's*

August 22, 2003, *Dialog Jumat, (Friday Dialogue)*, a 16-page insert read by Muslims to deepen knowledge of Islam before Friday prayers. All of those interviewed in the magazine's articles disassociated *Jemaah Islamiyah* (JI), the terrorist organization, from Islam.

In one of the *Dialog Jumat* articles, Muslim intellectual Professor Azyumardi Azra explained that, "*Jamaah Islamiyah* refers to the entire Islamic community. The only thing is, I think Muslims do not need to be emotional in confronting the West's accusation against JI, because what they mean by JI is a movement/organization, which according to intelligence information, is connected to various violent and terrorist acts...not the entire Islamic community."

In another article, based on an interview *Republika* conducted with me for that magazine, I am quoted as saying, "Indonesia and 50 other U.N. member countries have registered themselves as countries that agree that JI is a terrorist organization. Mention of JI has no connection with Islam. JI is a terrorist organization that has a political agenda of its own. I am certain that Islam will not justify terrorists' acts because I know that Islam is religion of peace."[58]

In subsequent years working in Indonesia, from 2006-2011, the same band of terrorists who attacked Bali twice, hotels in Jakarta twice and the Australian Embassy, would prove to be formidable adversaries for Indonesian security forces, carrying out many more attacks. While I was head of the U.S. Consulate in Medan, terrorists would attack police stations, shoot at the home where two American teachers lived in

Banda Aceh and set up a large terrorist training camp deep in the jungles of Aceh. They would be chased by police across Aceh.[59] A couple of terrorists fleeing from Aceh were shot by police a few blocks from my home in Medan, according to local media reports.

The U.S. and Indonesia have worked together in many areas to counter terrorism, including law enforcement, immigration, banking, and training of Indonesian counterterrorism police.

The war against terrorism in Indonesia has evolved into a police battle against criminals and the good guys are decisively winning the battle. I have no doubt that this fight will continue, but my gut feeling is that the chances of terrorists again being a major threat in Indonesia are minimal. I am not as confident about whether terrorist threats might escalate in some other parts of the world. Clearly, the world can learn from the tough yet humane approach that Indonesia has taken. �֍

PART THREE:

VALUES AND FAITH

SHARED VALUES

On October 2, 2001, as the U.S. image in the Muslim world began its plummet, the new Under Secretary of State for Public Diplomacy Charlotte Beers, an advertising executive known as the "Queen of Madison Avenue," began her difficult posting. She believed misunderstanding of the U.S., particularly in the Muslim world, was to blame for America's negative image. If only the world understood the U.S. better, then it would trust our policy, she believed.[60] America's diplomacy had failed to market the U.S. effectively, she contended. Under her leadership in 2001-2003, the U.S. Embassy in Jakarta undertook a campaign to "Brand America" to the world.

Funding for the programs to explain U.S. policy and promote the U.S. image abroad, administered by the State Department's Bureau of Public Diplomacy and Public Affairs (formerly USIA), had plummeted since the end of the Cold War in 1989. In Indonesia, facing budget cuts, we had closed the American Cultural Center and bilateral exchange programs had been drastically reduced in the 1990s. Reduction of these types of exchange programs over more than a decade resulted in a lost generation of important people-to-people exchanges that had helped the two nations understand each other.

Alumni of U.S. government-sponsored programs such as the Fulbright Scholarship Program and the International Visitor Leadership Program included many influential persons who were important in keeping open the lines of communications during rough times in bilateral relations from 2001 to 2008. These included Indonesian politicians Abdurrahman Wahid, Megawati Soekarnoputri and Amien Rais as well as Islamic scholars Nurcholish Madjid, Syafii Maarif, Azyumardi Azra and Anies Baswedan.

On the American side, the U.S. had sponsored graduate-level study, post graduate research, or speaking tours to Indonesia for such well-known scholars, business leaders and cultural experts as Bill Liddle, Robert Hefner, John Esposito, Don Emmerson, Doug Ramage, Jim Castle, Ed Van Ness and many others, all of whom contributed tremendously to bilateral goodwill. After 9/11, two of America's most prominent international affairs writers, Fareed Zakaria of *Time*

Magazine (now with CNN) and Thomas Friedman of *The New York Times,* visited Indonesia. Both have cited Indonesia frequently in their writings and commentaries as a positive example to the world of a Muslim majority democracy, promoting Indonesia's good image globally.[61] It is hard to imagine how the U.S. would have communicated with Indonesian leaders after September 11 without the goodwill that these people-to-people exchanges engendered.

Thus, the large increases in U.S. Public Diplomacy funding for Indonesia and across the world after September 11 was one blessing that came out of the ashes, an investment in friendship and scholarships that transcended the war against terrorism. The U.S. and Indonesia will always, from time to time, strongly disagree on certain policies. These are the times when personal relationships carry us across troubled waters.

In 2002, the U.S. Department of State launched the "Shared Values" campaign. Charlotte Beers' signature initiative to win the hearts and minds of the Muslim world was carried out in print, radio, television and with speakers. The premise was that if the U.S. could build trust with the Muslim world through common values then we could begin to chip away at negative views of the U.S. and its policies. Public opinion surveys revealed that the U.S. and the Muslim world both highly regarded several fundamental values: family, faith and learning.

One part of the initiative was "Muslim Life in America," an advertising campaign intended to convey that American Muslims are integrated into U.S. society, are successful, and have religious freedom. American Muslims, thus, were portrayed as both exemplifying American values such as entrepreneurship, educational achievement and freedom, while maintaining Muslim values as part of a religiously pluralistic America.

Our outreach to Muslims also included many real life interactions between people. The Ambassador and many other American officers at the Embassy hosted dinners to break the fast during the holy fasting month of Ramadan. Muslim Americans came on speaking tours to Indonesia and we sent Muslim groups to the U.S. Hundreds of teachers, *kiai* (Muslim boarding school headmasters) and students from *pesantren* (Muslim boarding schools) across Indonesia visited the U.S. I visited many of those *pesantren* years later, and found tremendous goodwill and understanding for the U.S. at the schools where students or staff had visited the U.S. We also funded mass Muslim organizations to promote tolerance and understanding, with good results. We supported not only Muslim organizations but also inter-religious initiatives, to promote tolerance among all religions.

One of the most powerful connections I experienced between Americans and Indonesian Muslims was through the music of the U.S. Muslim hip hop group "Remarkable Current," who I hosted in Padang, West Sumatra, and Medan, North Sumatra in 2010. They performed in Padang before 10,000 youth in an open field, one year after the earthquake that devastated West Sumatra. The Remarkable Current website quoted what I said at the time about the performances, "Their lyrics, music, movements and smiles transcended language barriers in a performance which combined the sanctity of Friday prayers with the electric charisma of a rock band."

Still, for the hundreds of audiences at schools and conferences across Indonesia that I have addressed since 2001, Indonesians were usually concerned with U.S. policy, not culture. They wanted to talk about the war against terrorism, Afghanistan, Iraq and Israel/Palestine. They were most interested in knowing what America does for world peace and welfare. Most importantly, they wanted to know that America was listening to their concerns.

In 2004, Chairman of West Sumatra's Muhammadiyah, Shofwan Karim, invited me to one of his *pesantren* to talk about U.S. society and policy. His bright students drilled me with questions about the war against terrorism, Israel and U.S. imperialism for two hours. Afterwards, these same students lined up by the hundreds to smile and shake my hand. One of them told me he had been so angry about U.S. foreign policy for so long that he was just happy to have a chance to confront "Uncle Sam" directly. My answers were not so important. The fact that I listened was what mattered.

President Bush visited Bali in October 2003 and had a positive meeting with five religious leaders. Bush told the media he did a lot of listening. The Indonesian religious figures in the meeting told the media afterwards that they criticized U.S. policy in Iraq, on Israel and regarding the perception that Americans

With Islamic high school students at the An Nur Pesantren, Bekasi, Java, June 10, 2004, during journalism training attended by 100 students from 45 pesantren in Jakarta, Bekasi and Tangerang.

equate Islam with terrorism. They were skeptical of Bush's responses but satisfied that he listened.

Words do matter. The rhetoric that Bush and his senior officials used throughout that administration bred distrust with the Muslim world and bigotry against Muslims by Americans. As U.S. Islamic scholar John Esposito points out, "Though Bush spoke of Muslims as a peaceful people and distinguished Islam from acts of terrorists immediately after 9/11, he simultaneously linked the Muslim world to terrorism."[62]

Bush's speeches and those of other senior White House officials almost always mentioned Muslims and terrorists in the same sentence. Bush coined the very unfortunate term "Islamofascism." Terms he repeated such as Islamic terrorism and Islamic extremism became part of the political vocabulary in the U.S.[63] It is no wonder that Indonesian Muslims felt attacked by the U.S. even as we asked for their sympathy in the war against terrorism.

Comparison of public opinion polls from 2000-2013 bears out that U.S. foreign policy in the Middle East created resentment among Indonesians while acts of kindness towards Indonesia created goodwill. As the chart below illustrates, a year before 9/11, before the U.S. was at war and during the time when the U.S. strongly supported Indonesia's democratic reform, U.S. popularity peaked. It then dove as the U.S. became involved in wars in Afghanistan and Iraq in 2002-2003, improved after the U.S. assisted Indonesia during the December 2004 tsunami, then rose much higher under a less military interventionist Obama administration that emphasized foreign assistance.[64]

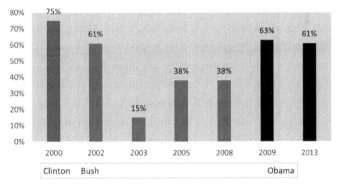

Indonesia Favorability Ratings of the U.S.

Of course, part of this trend was because Indonesians know Obama familiarly as, "*anak Menteng*" ("child of Menteng," a neighborhood in Jakarta where he attended school grades one through four), with 79 percent of Indonesians being aware of this fact.[65]

Personal relationships matter in Indonesia. For example, Paul Wolfowitz, despite his key role in the strategy to invade Iraq in 2003, is still well liked in Indonesia by those who remember his warmth and charisma as ambassador to Indonesia in 1986-89, when he enjoyed tremendous popularity. Interestingly, Wolfowitz's world view was likely influenced by his close relationship with Indonesia, a Muslim majority country that made a successful transition from autocracy to democracy. Perhaps Wolfowitz believed this same model could succeed in the Middle East.

Obama's foreign policy also played an important role in shaping Indonesians' opinions of the U.S. According to a 2009 Pew poll, 71 percent believed Obama would do the right thing in world affairs, 62 percent said he would consider the interests of Indonesia and 54 percent believed he would be fair in dealing with the Israeli-Palestinian conflict. On the other hand, at the same time Obama was implementing a troop surge in Afghanistan, 66 percent of Indonesians thought the U.S. and NATO should withdraw.[66]

President Obama's June 4, 2009, speech to the Muslim world in Cairo marked a new beginning for U.S.-Muslim world relations. The U.S. President expressed respect for Muslims and delinked Islam from terrorism in public statements. As I watched that speech with

Indonesian friends in Jakarta, the feeling of hope was palpable when Obama said, "I have come here to seek a new beginning between the United States and Muslims around the world; one based upon mutual interest and mutual respect; and one based upon the truth that America and Islam are not exclusive, and need not be in competition. Instead, they overlap, and share common principles – principles of justice and progress; tolerance and the dignity of all human beings." Notable in his speech was that he did not refer to terrorists or terrorism once.

My Indonesian friends, while still somewhat skeptical of U.S. intentions, also noted that the speech signified the U.S. would act less out of self-interest and more out of mutual interest. In the next couple of years, as I spoke before Muslim audiences, I was able to address non-political matters such as how to study in the U.S. and how American youth think, and not just contentious issues (the never-ending Palestine issue notwithstanding). In other words, I was able to focus more on positive stories of shared values and less on negative views of U.S. policy.

In the spirit of mutual interest and respect enunciated by Obama in Cairo, bilateral relations entered a new era with President Obama's visit to Indonesia in November 2010 and the announcement by Presidents Obama and Yudhoyono of the U.S.-Indonesia Comprehensive Partnership. This came to fruition under the U.S. Embassy leadership of Ambassador Cameron Hume, in close consultation with Indonesian leaders to ensure that the agreement fulfills bilateral aspirations.

The agreement set up six working groups to pursue cooperation in: Democracy and Civil Society, Education, Security, Environment and Climate, Energy, and Trade and Investment. The partnership has resulted in important cooperation on a wide range of issues, including health, science, technology, entrepreneurship and so forth. For example, in education, the agreement has resulted in greatly increased numbers of two-way scholarly exchanges, and cooperation to strengthen Indonesia's basic education system.[67]

As the Indonesian blogger Angga Kurniawan wrote, "In summary, the United States is carrying out its War on Terror in Indonesia through diplomacy and law enforcement, or a Soft Approach. This strategy is based on the desire for the two countries together to place principles of Democracy, balanced partnership, mutual respect, and shared values of freedom and tolerance as the foundation for cooperation."[68] ❀

RELIGIOUS FREEDOM

On July 28, 1764, James Harsha, my paternal ancestor, arrived in Stillwater, New York, on a boat of 300 Scotch-Irish immigrants. These Protestant Presbyterians, who called themselves "Seceders," had fled Ireland seeking religious and civil freedom. They had been persecuted by the English king for refusing to recognize the official Church of Ireland. James Harsha farmed the fertile American land and was a church elder. He fought in the United States War of Independence against the British to secure religious freedom for all Americans.

My mother, Genevieve, was a Christian who also believed in other world faiths, including Bahai, Hinduism, Buddhism, Islam and mysticism. She admired American Muslims who stood up for civil rights, such as Mohammad Ali and Malcolm X. As a young child in the 1960s, I went with her to peace demonstrations. In our home, we welcomed persons of all faiths, skin color and sexual orientation, for spirited discussions about religion, world peace and civil rights.

My mother raised me in a liberal Christian church, Divine Science, which followed the Unitarian-Universalism beliefs that Jesus Christ was not divine but rather divinely inspired, and with respect for the Prophet Mohammad. Founded in 1538 in Eastern Europe, Unitarians were the first Protestants to reject the Trinity of God, which they maintained was not found in the Bible. They believed that all people should be allowed to choose their faith.[69] Unitarians brought these tolerant views with them to America when they migrated in the 18th century. In colonial America, liberal Christians who believed in religious freedom struggled against conservative, Puritan Christians who wanted a monolithic practice of religion to be practiced in their settlements.

This conflict led one liberal Baptist preacher, Roger Williams, to leave the Puritan colony at Salem, Massachusetts, to found a new colony, Rhode Island, in 1636, where religious minorities were free to worship. The Colony of New York, influenced by liberal Dutch thinking and the diverse immigrants who settled there, also practiced religious freedom. Ultimately, liberal philosophy protecting religious freedom would be incorporated into the U.S. Constitution although the struggle between religiously tolerant and intolerant schools of thought would persist in the United States for centuries, until today.

During its colonial time, the United States population was dominated by white Protestants of Western European descent. There were few Jews and Catholics. There were probably tens of thousands of Muslims as well among the slaves transported from West Africa.[70] However, African American slaves had no freedom, and were forced to convert to Christianity by the plantation slave owners. By the time blacks were freed from slavery in 1865 and granted citizen rights in 1868, only a few managed to keep their Islamic faith. In the 20th century, many blacks would return to Islam (although the vast majority of African Americans are devout Christians).

American Protestants inherited their hostility towards Islam from 16th century Protestant reformers in Europe, who defined the Antichrist in terms of Islam. American Protestants were also bigoted towards the small minority of American Jews and Catholics.[71]

However, some liberal Protestants, including Unitarians, Universalists, Deists and some clergy of several other religions, such as Baptists, had a tolerant attitude towards Islam. In addition, several of America's most influential founding fathers, including Thomas Jefferson and James Madison, were strong defenders of freedom of religion for all faiths, including Islam.

In fact, Thomas Jefferson owned an annotated 1764 version of the Koran translated into English, which he studied carefully. His concept of religious freedom, written into the U.S. Constitution in 1787, was intended to be inclusive of Islam, Catholicism, Judaism and even atheism. Jefferson even studied Arabic. In his home state of Virginia, he drafted the "Bill for Establishing Religious Freedom" to protect "the Jew and the Gentile, the Christian and the Mahometan (Muslim), the Hindoo and infidel of every denomination."

Jefferson was influenced by the 17th century English political philosopher John Locke.[72] In his seminal "Letter on Toleration," John Locke wrote that Muslims and all others who believed in God should be tolerated in England. He argued that religious intolerance by Christians is both unchristian and irrational.[73]

Denise Spellberg, an American historian who wrote a book on this topic, wrote, "At a time when most Americans were uninformed, misinformed, or simply afraid of Islam, Thomas Jefferson imagined Muslims as future citizens of his new nation. His engagement with the faith began with the purchase of a Qur'an eleven years before he wrote the Declaration of Independence."[74]

Interestingly, Jefferson's political enemies claimed he was a Muslim because of his tolerant beliefs.[75]

Despite guarantee of freedom of religion under the First Amendment of the Constitution,[76] the battle for non-Protestants and non-whites to win acceptance in the U.S. would be a painful and slow civil rights battle, from the nation's founding in 1776 until today. As the numbers of non-Protestant groups increased "each would be branded as foreign and a threat to the Government of the United States." Eventually, Jews and Catholics would win acceptance in the latter half of the 20th century, "but Muslims would be the last to struggle for inclusion."[77]

The U.S. census system cannot ask people their religion, so there are no accurate figures on the numbers of Muslims in the U.S., but various reliable estimates range from between three and six million American Muslims[78] in a population of 300 million Americans. The vast majority of Muslims immigrated to the U.S. after 1965, when a new immigration law allowed for immigrants to come from diverse parts of the world. This law opened up the door for large numbers of Muslims to come to America from the Middle East and South Asia. According to a Pew study, the proportion of Muslim Americans who are foreign born is 65 percent.[79]

Of the 35 percent of Muslim Americans who are indigenous, 40 percent are African Americans, who reverted to what they perceived as their original faith. American Muslim converts are diverse, with large percentages of blacks, whites, Asians, and Hispanics.[80] The largest ethnic Muslim group is from South Asia (Pakistan, India and Bangladesh). Other significant Muslim immigrant populations came from the Middle East, Malaysia and Indonesia, with large numbers also from Turkey, Eastern Europe and many African countries.[81] Among the large numbers of foreign born Muslims, 81 percent have won citizenship.[82] Muslim immigrants are dispersed across America.

As for varieties of Islam, 65 percent identify as Sunnis, 11 percent profess Shi'ism and 24 percent refuse to be classified.[83] Sufism also plays an important role in America. The Ahmadiyya community has been very active in the work of *da'wa* (missionary work), with Ahmadi centers in more than 50 cities in the U.S. and Canada. (Ahmadis' identification as Islamic is challenged by many Muslims.)

"American Muslims represent the most ethnically, racially, and theologically diverse Islamic community in the world," wrote Spellberg.[84] American Muslims have higher achievements in education and income than average Americans[85] and Muslims who immigrate to America tend to be well educated.

One of the most important issues for American Muslims is education, including Islamic parochial education for children and mosque instruction. The number of private Islamic schools in America is growing but there are still only 250. An important concern is "educating American Muslims Islamic ethics and equipping them to lead morally responsible lives."[86]

Celebrating American holidays is important for cultural assimilation in the U.S. Thanksgiving is appreciated by Muslim Americans as an Islamic event in that it is a day to reflect on God's bounty, shared with family and friends. Christmas is the most problematical for American Muslims since it is such an important time to share with American friends.[87] Some Muslims in the U.S. will not celebrate Christmas at all while others will share Christmas greetings with Christian friends and attend Christmas social gatherings.

Because I was socialized in the liberal and secular beliefs of Thomas Jefferson and Unitarians, I found a comfortable spiritual home in Indonesia. During my life, I have worshipped in evangelical churches in Arkansas and Batak churches in Sumatra, kissed the Pope's hand in Venezuela, meditated at Buddhist temples in Tibet and at Hindu temples in Bali, and bowed in prayer at mosques across Indonesia and Malaysia. On many occasions, I have attended prayer and meditation sessions in Indonesia holding hands with Muslims and persons of all faiths. The call to prayer is the most beautiful song I hear before dawn and the most peaceful sound at dusk.

Indonesia is similar to the U.S. in being a secular society that protects freedom of religion. Indonesia also is similar in that the vast majority of Indonesians are tolerant with a small number being hostile to other faiths. In fact, I find that religious tolerance or intolerance among the 87 percent of Indonesians who are Muslim to be similar to attitudes of the 78 percent of Americans who are Christian. American Muslims face some of the same issues faced by Christian Indonesians in terms of assimilation into society.

I once had a conversation about religion and culture in Indonesia with the writer and journalist Mohamad Sobary, who explained about the history of the past two centuries of Islamic religious fundamentalism and nationalism in Indonesia and how fundamentalists have never constituted more than a small minority in Indonesia. Several Indonesian scholars I have spoken with basically agree that at least 80 percent of Indonesians are moderate, less than 20 percent are conservative, only a few percent are extreme, and a very small, unknown number of fanatics are violent. There are no violent Muslims in Indonesia, only violent people who have lost all faith.

Robert Hefner describes how Indonesia's particular brand of "civil Islam" resulted in democracy and respect for human rights under democratic *reformasi*.[88] The Indonesian Islamic scholar, Azyumardi Azra, explains how this type of moderate Muslim culture represents "Islam with a smiling face" and that it is so dominant in the history and culture of Indonesia, that "it is almost a myth that the Islamists would be able to wrestle political power" in Indonesia.[89] "Moderate Islam in Indonesia is too big to fail," he said at a November 2014 conference in Aceh that I attended.

More importantly, religion has been a unifying factor that has promoted democracy and defended human rights in Indonesia. Where would democracy and human rights be without the moderate and pro-*reformasi* (democratic reformation) mass religious organizations of Nahdlatul Ulama (NU) and Muhammadiyah, and without Muslim leaders such as Gus Dur, Amien Rais, Syafii Maarif and Nurcholish Madjid. Islam has been the major driving force behind democracy and freedom in Indonesia.

The roots of religious-based conflict in Indonesia, more often than not, are political or cultural. The political actors are many and their motives diverse— power, land, wealth and so forth—but seldom has the real cause been faith.

In fact, Islam in Indonesia is the most important influence for unity and tolerance. "Islam in Indonesia has many colored flowers, it has many different practices," Azyumardi Azra said in November 2014, adding, "Indonesians cannot live with Wahhabism."

Any approach to extremism in Indonesia needs to address, foremost, economic and social issues. In the words of NU Chairman Ahmad Syafii Maarif, "The luster of fundamentalism in Indonesia is more due to national failure to meet the aspirations of freedom to build social justice and create prosperity for the people."[90] ✺

CULTURAL RACISM

Ibrahim Kalin, Georgetown University scholar, writes about cultural racism, which defines individuals through their culture, defining some cultures in positive ways and others in bigoted ways. He writes, "Exaggerating cultural differences to the point of moral incompatibility is a tactic often employed by cultural conservatives to maintain a certain imagery of European or Western civilization. The same mistake is also committed by Muslim groups in the name of political opposition and resistance."[91]

While majorities of Indonesians and Americans are tolerant, I am very concerned about hardening of views by cultural conservatives in both Indonesia and the U.S. Since 9/11, I have personally had many anguishing discussions with friends and family in both the U.S. and Indonesia regarding culture and religion.

In the U.S., I have been disturbed by hateful statements about Islam and foreign cultures. While I can have rational discussions about Islam with most people, some people I know immediately begin to talk about how Islam is a religion of violence.

In Indonesia, I have felt increasingly uncomfortable with intolerant attitudes. A few pious Muslims have refused to shake my hand and reciprocate the Muslim greeting "*assalamualaikum*" assuming that I am not a Muslim, and despite the fact that there is nothing in Islam that prevents Muslims greeting persons of different faiths. Some Indonesian Muslims now refuse to say Merry Christmas to their Christian fellow citizens.

In the U.S., views of Islam are increasingly polarized, with liberal Democrats having much more favorable views towards Muslims than do conservative Republicans. Younger, better educated and more liberal Americans see Muslims favorably, while older, less educated, white Evangelical protestants have the most negative views, according to a 2007 Pew Research poll,[92] a trend that has continued according to a 2014 Pew poll.

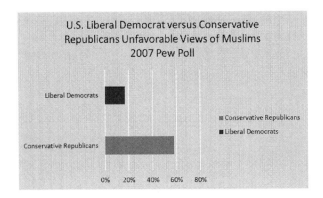

Prejudices against Muslims are reinforced with lies issued daily by conservative political pundits and far right religious leaders. These same far right pundits also defame Obama, perhaps because he is black, maybe because he is liberal, or possibly because he has a foreign sounding name. One far right Christian website even accused Obama of manufacturing the Ebola virus to massacre Christians, saying the "bo" in Ebola is code for Barack Obama!

On the other hand, I also have attended interfaith dialogues in the U.S. packed with audiences who want to understand Islam and other faiths. Almost all the many university campuses I have visited across the U.S. in recent years are seeking more Muslim students, have prayer rooms on campus with mosques nearby, and serve halal food in the cafeterias. My son socializes at his college with a group of close friends (including Indonesians) who are Christians, Muslims and of other faiths. Whenever they are all together, no one drinks liquor out of respect for the Muslims.

Some statistics about how Americans and Indonesians view Islam-West relations are revealing. The vast majority of Americans believe greater Muslim-West interactions are a benefit while Indonesians have more mixed feelings about this issue, as illustrated by the graph below.[93]

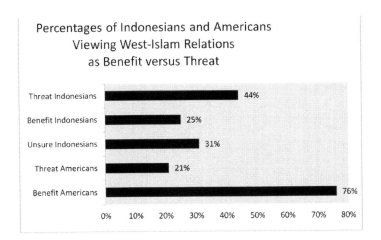

Percentages of Indonesians and Americans
Viewing West-Islam Relations
as Benefit versus Threat

These figures likely mean that Americans want the Muslim world to like and understand them.

Indonesians, on the other hand, might still feel threatened by the West, both politically and culturally, or simply are ambivalent. For example, a 2013 Pew survey revealed that Indonesians are open to modernization and science but are more guarded about Western cultural influences, as the chart below illustrates.[94]

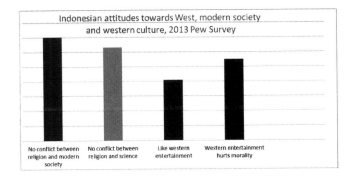

Understandably, Indonesians want to fully participate in a modern, technological world but are concerned about maintaining their own traditions and values in the face of values portrayed by Hollywood and other Western moral values that could erode Indonesian traditions. Indonesia's younger population is pulled between piety and materialism, call to prayer and discos, the Koran and Facebook, shadow puppet plays and Hollywood.

Americans do not know much about Islam but are largely tolerant. While 35 percent believe Islam encourages more violence than do other religions, an increase from 25 percent since 2002, 62 percent of Americans believe Muslims should have the same rights as other groups to build houses of worship in local communities.[95]

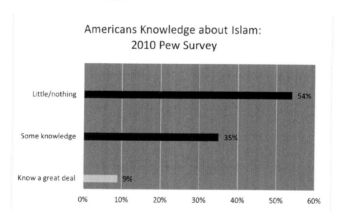

By comparison, Indonesian Muslims do not know much about Christianity and support sharia law, but reject extremism. According to a 2013 Pew Research polling in Indonesia:

- Only 12 percent of Indonesian Muslims were knowledgeable about Christianity.
- Only 9 percent had attended an interfaith meeting.
- Almost all Muslims, 95 percent, said most or all their friends are Muslim.
- 87 percent said Islam and Christianity are very different.
- 72 percent wanted sharia to be the law of the land.
- 50 percent said sharia should also apply to non-Muslims.

However, Indonesians also expressed sentiments supporting tolerance, peace and democratic values:

- 92 percent believed suicide bombing is not justified.
- 53 percent worried about religious extremism and 36 percent said religious conflict is a big problem.
- 61 percent favored democracy over a strong leader.[96]

As is the case in the U.S., Indonesians have a strong reservoir of tolerance but much can still be done to promote understanding among religions. It is best to begin at a young age with civic education in school that teaches about all religions and emphasizes teaching tolerance through exercises. Children can engage with persons of other faiths to learn what they have in common. In the U.S., all children should be taught about Islamic culture and history, as part of their general education. (When I was in school, I learned nothing about Islamic civilization until I attended college).

Regrettably, the vast majority of Indonesian Muslims are anti-Semitic. Every time I speak to audiences, most of the discussion time is spent talking about the Israeli-Palestinian conflict and refuting Indonesians' irrational views that there is a Jewish/CIA conspiracy to destroy Islam. This discussion with Indonesians is exhausting and leads nowhere. I strongly agree that Indonesians should condemn the Israeli government's cruel attacks on Palestinian civilians but believe they also should criticize hardliners on both sides, including Hamas, whose actions are also provoking conflict.

Americans support Israel because of close historical ties with Israel and because of America's respect for Jews and Judaism (although more Jews in the U.S. are victims of hate crimes each year than are Muslims).[97] On the other hand, Americans also are divided over Israeli government actions in Palestine. Over half of young people and nearly half of Democrats and Independents say Israel is unjustified in its attacks against Palestinians that occurred in the middle of 2014,[98] and liberal American Jews (most Jews are Democrats) join in condemning the Israeli government policy while still supporting Israel.

Clearly, a new approach is needed to solve the Israeli-Palestine conflict, particularly one which addresses violent actions by the Israeli government against Palestinian civilians. Until this happens, the Middle East problem will continue to severely hurt Indonesian perceptions of the U.S.

However, Indonesians also could play a much more constructive role in helping to end the suffering and conflict in Palestine if they would rethink their anti-Semitic biases and try to engage both sides of the conflict. Indonesia is in a unique position to play a major role if it is willing to also engage Israel.

In fact, Indonesia is a leading world model for a peaceful, tolerant and modern multi-religious society. More Indonesians of all faiths should travel as emissaries of peace and understanding to the U.S. to convey how a Muslim majority country with over 300 ethnic groups and over a thousand years of multi-religious harmony has forged a progressive and democratic country.

Jusuf Wanandi, a senior Indonesian political analyst, wrote in 2001, "There is a strong belief in many quarters within and without of the country that a modern, open, democratic and economically viable Indonesia can become a model for other Muslim countries. Indeed, Indonesia can become a model where Islam has self-confidence and is on par with the West and other developed nations."[99] ❋

ARE WE CHARLIE HEBDO?

The January 6, 2015, terrorist murder of 12 people in the *Charlie Hebdo* office was France's 9/11 or Bali bombing. French citizens and people worldwide united against this terror with the rallying call, *Je suis Charlie*, "I am Charlie." However, for Muslims, and many non-Muslims, who found *Charlie Hebdo's* satire offensive, declaring solidarity with *Charlie Hebdo* was an ethical dilemma. Clearly, regardless of how offended Muslims or members of other religions were by *Charlie Hebdo*, violent attacks against freedom of information are not justified. However, the objective of this chapter is not to discuss freedom of expression but rather how

Charlie Hebdo relates to the larger issue of respect and dignity for Islam.

The *Charlie Hebdo* attack and other terrorist threats across Europe succeeded in terrifying hundreds of millions of people in Europe and around the world. The terrorists also succeeded in further isolating populations of peace loving Muslims in Western nations. Media commentary following the attack played into the terrorists' hands, further sowing fear and division between Muslims and non-Muslims.

Following the Paris attacks, American news broadcasters such as Fox News and CNN repeatedly asked why Muslims are not taking a stand against such terrorist acts. This was despite the fact that influential Muslims throughout the world immediately and vehemently condemned the Paris attack. The media ignored statements such as that by the Council on American-Islamic Relations (CAIR), which said, "We strongly condemn this brutal and cowardly attack and reiterate our repudiation of any such assault on freedom of speech, even speech that mocks faith and religious figures. The proper response to such attacks on the freedoms we hold dear is not to vilify any faith, but instead to marginalize extremists of all backgrounds who seek to stifle freedom and to create or widen societal divisions."[100]

American news stations paraded out "terrorism experts," many of them retired U.S. generals now working in the security or defense industries, who alarmed audiences with opinions about the danger of Islamic extremism, outlining military solutions.

These "experts" claimed to understand the terrorists' motives before the criminals were even clearly identified. As John Horgan, Director of the Center for Terrorism and Security Studies at the University of Massachusetts Lowell, explains in his thoughtful 2014 book, "Contemporary debate is replete with 'terrorism experts,' perhaps as confusing a term as it is misleading when one listens to 'analysis' that is foolishly rushed out sometimes minutes after a terrorist attack. Being first, it seems, is better than being right, especially when speculative accounts are rarely held up after events prove them wrong."[101]

In addition, influential American analysts publicly called for Muslims worldwide to take a public stand against this terrorist attack, as if the world's 1.6 billion Muslims should apologize for the acts of a few terrorists who falsely used Islam. Media tycoon Rupert Murdoch, owner of Fox News, said, "Maybe most Muslims are peaceful, but until they recognize and destroy their growing jihadist cancer they must be held responsible."[102]

In the U.S., prominent Muslims and politically moderate non-Muslims questioned why Muslims are responsible for the acts of misguided terrorists. They asked whether all Christians should be responsible for terrorist acts by a few deviant Christians. For example, the Norwegian Anders Behring Breivik massacred 77 persons in Norway in a politically motivated, anti-Islam attack, inspired by his deranged interpretation of Christianity.[103]The Ku Klux Klan (KKK), a white, Protestant Christian organization in the U.S., has carried out countless acts of terrorism against blacks, including the 1963 bombing of a Baptist Church in Birmingham, Alabama, killing four young girls. Christians condemn these attacks but Christianity is not held responsible.

Following the Paris attacks and other terrorism acts by Muslims against Western countries, many politicians and media commentators in the U.S. associated these attacks with Islam. However, there are too many complex reasons for why a few people become terrorists, and religion is not the cause. For example, a teenager in my home state of Colorado in 2014 was arrested and sent to prison because of her plans to leave the U.S. to marry a member of the Islamic State in Iraq and Syria (ISIS) and support terrorism. She was an immature teenage girl who made a foolish decision which she now regrets. She probably knew little of the Koran and nothing could have prevented her juvenile fantasy.

As the U.S. terrorist psychology expert John Horgan wrote, "American jihadists are an incredibly diverse group. They include all levels of economic success and failure and every sort of background and ethnicity, including blacks and whites, Latinos, women and even Jews. They come from big cities and small towns and every part of America, including the East and West Coasts, the Deep South, and the Midwest." He explained that in one study of thousands of terrorists, "no two radicals were the same." He added, "Terrorist motivation is defined by its complexity, and once again attempts to provide an overall explanation for all terrorists are utterly meaningless."[104]

In his study of the 9/ 11 terrorists and those who worked closely with them—five hundred people in all—forensic psychiatrist Marc Sageman found that only 25 percent had a traditional Islamic upbringing; that two-thirds were secularly minded until they encountered al-Qaeda; and the rest were recent converts. Their knowledge of Islam was therefore limited. Many were self-taught, and some would not study the Quran thoroughly until they were in prison. Perhaps, Sageman concludes, the problem was not Islam but ignorance of Islam.[105]

Karen Armstrong, one of U.S.'s foremost writers about religion and Islam, makes valid points about current attitudes towards terrorism and Islam in the West. First, she points out that in "religious history, the struggle for peace has been just as important as the holy war." She explains that throughout history, all religions are political and used to justify violence, Christianity and Islam included. However, religions are also forces for peace and humanity.

Second, Armstrong writes, "Only a tiny proportion of fundamentalists commit acts of terror; most are simply trying to live a devout life in a world that seems increasingly hostile to faith, and nearly all begin with what is perceived as an assault on them by the secular, liberal establishment."[106]

Many Westerners blame Islam for terrorist threats spreading from countries that are failed states, such as Iraq, Syria, Yemen, Nigeria and Somalia. Divine causes are hardly to blame for broken societies. Of course, the threat coming from Iraq is the direct result of the U.S.'s disastrous attempt to export American democracy to Iraq.

CIA torture of Muslims, unlawful imprisonment of innocent Muslims, and large scale killing of innocent civilians by the U.S. military in Iraq and Afghanistan, only help terrorists to recruit American Muslims. Some studies have suggested that Muslims are most moved by stories of the suffering of Muslims, which is human nature and applies equally to Christians. As Armstrong writes, "We routinely and rightly condemn the terrorism that kills civilians in the name of God, but we cannot claim the high moral ground if we dismiss the suffering and death of the many thousands of civilians who die in our wars as 'collateral damage'."[107]

John Esposito, Islamic Studies professor at Georgetown University in Washington, D.C., wrote, "Avoiding or ending acute conflicts in the Muslim world is more effective than projecting a strong military presence to safeguard American interests and limit the growth of global terrorism. The argument that a strong military presence in the region will win the war against terrorism is not borne out by Gallup data from across the Muslim world. The long war against terror will not be won on the battlefield, but by winning the loyalty of the people in the region. While terrorists must be fought aggressively, military occupation of Muslim lands increases anti-American sentiment, diminishes American moral authority with allies, and silences the voices of moderates who want better relations."[108]

In the U.S. and Europe, the biggest concern today is that ISIS, al-Qaeda and other terrorist organizations are recruiting citizens of Western countries. In that case, law enforcement and military solutions are only stopgap measures which will never reach the thousands of misguided youth being radicalized in Internet chat rooms.

While the U.S. and Europe both face much work to counter alienation of their Muslim populations, Europe has a much more serious problem than the U.S. There are "two major features of Muslims in Europe that stand in sharp contrast to the features of Muslims in the United States: European Muslims are mostly immigrants. European Muslims are socioeconomically marginalized."[109]

As President Obama advised European leaders on January 15, 2015, "Our biggest advantage (over Europe)...is that our Muslim populations, they feel themselves to be Americans. And there is this incredible process of immigration and assimilation that is part of our tradition that is probably our greatest strength." He added, "It's important for Europe to not simply respond with a hammer and law enforcement and military approaches to these problems."[110]

While I am thankful that Obama has the empathy to respect Muslims, he must do much more to build bridges with American Muslims. Yvonne Haddad, Professor of Islamic History at the University of Massachusetts, explains, "9/11 focused American attention on Arab

Photo: U.S. Embassy Jakarta

Me, as U.S. Embassy Jakarta Press Attaché, with daughter Annisa (to my left), and U.S. Embassy Jakarta staff, with U.S. Secretary of State Colin Powell, in the U.S. Embassy courtyard, August 8, 2002.

and Muslim Americans. It precipitated the passage of the Patriot Act, which stripped them of the protection of constitutional guarantees. It sanctioned without notification the monitoring of bank transactions, telephone conversations, e-mail messages, books purchased or borrowed from libraries, credit card purchases, and so on. It brought an end to political correctness. Demonizing Islam and Muslims became acceptable, a fact that has spawned the Islamophobia industry, with individuals and organizations profiting from speaking and writing about the threat of their presence."[111]

Esposito writes, "Diagnosing terrorism as a symptom and Islam as the problem, though popular in some circles, is flawed and has serious risks with dangerous repercussions. It confirms radical beliefs and fears, alienates the moderate Muslim majority, and reinforces a belief that the war against global terrorism is really a war against Islam. Whether one is radical or moderate, this negative attitude is a widespread perception."[112]

He also points out that, "The problem is not Islam any more than Christianity or Judaism is the cause of its extremists and terrorists; it's the political radicalization of religion that creates militant theologies. Islam may be a powerful weapon for discrediting terrorists and limiting the growth of terrorism. For example, in Indonesia, those who say that 9/11 was unjustified support this response by citing religious principles ("It is against God's law," "God hates murder," or "It is against Islam") as well as humanitarian ones (the loss of human life was tragic, and so forth), while those who say that 9/11 was justified cite political grievances to support their response, not religious justifications."[113]

On a positive note, American Muslims and a large number of non-Muslim Americans are working towards tolerance. As Haddad explains, the Muslim community is opening its mosques to the general public, is involved in interfaith activities and is talking about pluralism. Despite the risk of being attacked by far right Christians for speaking out, more Muslims are countering Islamophobic false accusations and seeking redress in the courts against discrimination. She adds that her "surveys show that they love the country and want to be active productive citizens....They believe in the promise of America—"out of many, one"—and believe that just as once-reviled Catholics and Jews have been accepted as constituent members of the nation, the day is not far off when Islam and Muslims will also be accepted.[114]

The February 10, 2015, murder of three Muslim American students in Chapel Hill, North Carolina, shocked the U.S. Thousands of mourners turned out in Chapel Hill in support of the three young Muslims with such promising futures. The killer, an atheist, may have been influenced by Islamophobia or perhaps was simply an angry and violent man. Police and the FBI will investigate whether this was a hate crime.

However, the national media in the U.S. reported the murders with great empathy for Muslims. CNN even broadcast the entire Azan prayers. Muslim Americans, frightened by these murders, spoke out against Islamophobia. My sense is that Americans are listening. Sometimes it takes a horrible act of racial violence to make Americans think about tolerance. I believe these murders will lead to more dialogue and understanding of American Muslims.

America must protect the civil liberties of its Muslims not only to worship but also to be free to express themselves. Americans must be free to counter lies about Islam and to criticize the U.S. government when it violates the civil liberties of Muslims. This battle is not only for Muslims but for the rights of all Americans. I worry that the current open-ended "war against terrorism" threatens the very liberties that Thomas Jefferson espoused over 200 hundred years ago, and which my ancestor James Harsha fought to defend. ✸

LEARNING FROM WISE
INDONESIANS

I have been enriched by interactions with Indonesians of all faiths over the past 28 years. Following are some of my favorite persons and moments.

I was fortunate enough to have private conversations with two of Indonesia's greatest writers, Mochtar Lubis (1922-2004) and Pramoedya Ananta Toer (1925-2006), both of whom contributed to Indonesia's transition towards a more honest, freed and fair society.

Lubis, born in West Sumatra, was an investigative journalist and novelist of world renown. He told me a little about his life when we met in Jakarta in

1987. During his youth, he taught school in Nias and trekked into the jungles of North Sumatra where he had a close call with a tiger. A critic of President Soekarno, he was imprisoned by him. His most well-known novel, *Twilight in Jakarta (Senja di Jakarta)*, was the first Indonesian novel to be translated into English. Taking place in the early 1950s, its story about corruption, inequality and immoral politicians still resonates in Indonesia today. Lubis also was imprisoned by Soeharto in 1974, and his newspaper, *Indonesia Raya*, was shut down in 1975. Lubis told me about his hope for press freedom and democracy to take hold in Indonesia. In 2000, he was named as one of the International Press Institute's 50 World Press Heroes in the past 50 years.

Two years before he passed away, Henny and I spent an afternoon at the home of Indonesia's most persecuted and celebrated novelist and journalist, Pramoedya Ananta Toer. A left wing supporter of Soekarno, he was imprisoned on Buru Island by Soeharto in 1965. During his 14 years there, denied pencil and paper, he composed orally his *Buru Quartet* novels about Indonesian nationalism, recognized as one of the world's greatest works of literature. Henny and I sat with him in his living room in 2004, and listened to him expound on how he believes that Javanese-dominated Indonesian society is hopelessly feudal and corrupt. Chain smoking clove (*kretek*) cigarettes, he extolled the virtues of Soekarno. He then took us for a walk in his large garden, which he planted entirely himself in his late 70s, his dream after half a lifetime of imprisonment. Living only with his wife, he did not have a gardener or servant.

Henny and I with writer Pramoedya Ananta Toer, at his home in Bogor, 2004, when he was 79 years old.

I met my friend, Fadhil Lubis, when I interviewed him for a Fulbright Scholarship to study Islam at the University of California in Los Angeles in 1989. Pak Fadhil and I used to travel together for days at a time across Sumatra, discussing religion. He got his doctorate from UCLA on a Fulbright scholarship. Now rector of the National Institute of Islamic Religion (IAIN) in Medan, Fadhil is one of Indonesia's great Islamic and inter-religious scholars, a beacon of teaching tolerance for IAIN students.

Shofwan Karim, Rector of Muhammadiyah University West Sumatra, is another good friend and also one of the leading religious scholars in Indonesia. Muhammadiyah is the flesh, blood and soul of West Sumatra. Shofwan's success lies in his entrepreneurial skills, using business to fund *pesantren*, and in teaching students modern, practical skills so that they can earn a living after they graduate. West Sumatra's real wealth is its people, so the children have to be smart to succeed.

The first time I visited West Sumatra in 1987, I saw what I believed at the time to be the largest *pesantren* in West Sumatra, with 20,000 students. They all lined up to greet me, girls on one side and boys on the other. The students lived in pairs in huts, no bigger than a Hobbit's bedroom. I had to stoop to enter one.

I also had the pleasure of knowing the late Nurcholish Madjid, known affectionately as Cak Nur, one of the great intellectuals in Indonesia's history who contributed to unifying Indonesians of all faiths through his vision. He once wrote, "In understanding the Koran's teaching about the correct path it is clear that fundamentally it points to a path that is used by all religions from all prophets that has to be upheld by their followers."[115] His successor as rector of Paramadina Institute, Anies Baswedan, has carried the mantel of Cak Nur. He was named one of the top young leaders of the world by several international organizations. In 2014, he was appointed by President Jokowi as the Minister of Basic Education.

I love inter-religious dialogue and no nation does this with more fervor and sincerity than does Indonesia, where leaders of all faiths come together at important times to resolve conflict and appeal for peace, including leaders of all the six official faiths. For example, in 2004, a delegation of 24 representatives of Indonesia's five largest religions—Muslim, Catholic, Protestant, Buddhist and Hindu — visited the Vatican to affirm their commitment for world peace.

I used to meet regularly with members of the Forum for Harmony Among Religions in Medan. This group, representing all the major religions, could openly discuss difficult issues of religious conflict and resolve them. For example, they traveled as a group to one remote part of North Sumatra to look into an attack on a church there and bring about peaceful resolution. They told me that people of different faiths in North Sumatra get along better than anywhere in Indonesia because North Sumatra is so equally divided among religions and ethnicities that people have learned to get along with each other.

Indonesia Church Forum (FGI) also has also proven to be a very important organization, both in terms of dialogue with Muslim organizations, and in defending the rights of Christians against extremists. In fact, some Christians are terrified of being attacked by fringe hate groups in Indonesia, and FGI has been active in reaching out to society to create understanding. The Islamic Defenders Front (FPI) has been especially successful in stirring up attacks against churches in communities where Christians had been living in harmony with Muslims. One brave Christian leader I know even used to be in contact with Abu Bakar Ba'asyir in the hope of persuading him to prevent attacks against Christians. In Indonesia, this friend explained, Christian leaders have to come to an understanding even with radicals to protect their parishioners.

Din Syamsuddin, as chair of the Centre for Dialogue and Cooperation Among Civilizations (CDCC), has done great work to increase international tolerance, bringing together leaders of all faiths for meaningful discussions, even inviting rabbis.

Similarly, the Wahid Institute under the leadership of Yenny Wahid and Ahmad Suaedy has been at the forefront of promoting tolerance and pushing the envelope of inter-religious harmony in the spirit of the Wahid Institute founder Gus Dur, also reaching out to Judaism. Both the CDCC and the Wahid Institute have hosted many wonderful international conferences to discuss peace and tolerance.

In addition, universities and religious organizations across Indonesia regularly hold conferences on themes related to inter-religious and Islam-West dialogue. The Indonesian scholars at these conferences are typically the most universal in their thinking, compared to speakers from other countries.

Ahmad Fuadi, the journalist and author of a bestselling autobiographical novel made into a hit movie, Country of Five Towers (*Negeri Lima Menara*), is known for bringing positive portrayals of Indonesian *pesantren* to the world. He is one of many examples of Indonesian graduates of *pesantren* who are progressive moderate thinkers. I have visited over 50 *pesantren* and realize the important contributions they make to preparing educated and moral young men and women who are open to global thinking. All the *pesantren* I visited in recent years teach at least two foreign languages, English and Arabic, so that the youth are prepared to interact in two worlds.

In his novel, Ahmad wrote a touching story about receiving an Indonesian-American English conversation book from Voice of America (VOA) which made such a difference in his life. "It felt good to know that this world was listening and responding to me." Ahmad wrote that the VOA broadcaster Abdul Nur Adnan show, "Islam in America," had given him a realization that there are mosques in America and that students from Muslim countries go to American campuses to gain the latest knowledge. Determined to study in America, he wrote as a young student, "*Man jadda wajada*" ("Whoever truly believes will succeed"). He would later get his master's degree in the U.S. on a Fulbright scholarship and has since returned to the U.S. to talk to Americans about the modern, tolerant nature of Islam in Indonesia. He is an inspiration to all Indonesian youth of what they can accomplish through determination and faith. ✿

PART FOUR

DEMOCRACY AND HUMAN RIGHTS: ONE FALLS, A THOUSAND OTHERS GROW[116]

View from Above
Beautiful Mini
Indonesia Park

W hen I arrived in Indonesia in August 1986, the first place I visited was the Beautiful Mini Indonesia Park (*Taman Mini Indonesia Indah*), a microcosm of Indonesia at a time when Soeharto's power was beginning its slow decline. Having just arrived in Jakarta and already enchanted with Indonesia, I strolled among the 26 miniature provinces each represented by a traditional house, visited the park's mosque, Catholic church, Protestant church, and Hindu and Buddhist temples, and took the tram to soar above the mini-archipelago lake and islands.

Taman Mini symbolized Indonesia's *Bhineka Tunggal Ika* (Unity in Diversity), or, as the U.S. describes the same concept, *E Pluribus Unum* (Out of Many, One). Each province was picture perfect. Taman Mini epitomized the world's political view of Indonesia at that time.

By 1986, Indonesia had risen out of extreme poverty and starvation in just one generation under Soeharto. By the 1980s, the economy was humming along at six percent annual growth. Highrises and shopping centers were mushrooming along Jakarta's Jalan Sudirman corridor. The luxury Nusa Dua resort in Bali opened up that paradise to foreign tourists. At every remote village I traveled to in the next few years, people would praise newly installed electricity lines and paved roads. Even in remote jungle villages, families gathered at food stalls (*warung*) each night to watch TV Republik Indonesia (TVRI), the nation's only television station, thanks to the *Palapa* satellite that transmitted daily images of Soeharto and his generals commissioning new hospitals and opening up factories. On Martin Luther King Day in February 1988, I watched TVRI in a jungle logging camp in North Sumatra, where the *warung* owner commented on the American civil rights martyr Martin Luther King, saying, "Oh, I didn't know Martin Luther King was still alive!"

In a 1986 story featured in the media, Soeharto is shown inspecting condoms at a factory, part of the enormously successful "two children is enough" family planning campaign that used social pressure to control

Indonesia's population. One could ask almost anyone in those days how many children they had, and get the answer, "Two is enough."

Soeharto's regime had contributed greatly to Indonesian prosperity and social welfare during his first 20 years in power, and he was still popular. This would unravel only slowly during the next 15 years as people's expectations rose.

What I did not see during my tram ride above Taman Mini was that Ibu Tien, or "Mrs. 10 percent" as they called her for her custom of taking the top 10 percent of every public project, had used a foundation to build the park at an enormous cost, siphoning off large amounts of public funds. In the coming years, her children also would enrich themselves from charitable foundations. I also did not know about the many farmers who had been forced to sell their land at half its value to make room for this fantasyland. I was not aware of the student protests against the project when it opened in 1975, a rare occurrence in the Soeharto era.[117]

Soeharto's repressive techniques were effective enough that protests or media criticism were rare. Government crackdowns were kept quiet. My journalist friends in Jakarta, who occasionally pushed the envelope by printing mildly critical views of the Indonesian government, were forced out of their jobs or saw their publications shut down. For example, in 1986, *Sinar Harapan* newspaper was closed and Chief Editor Aristides ("Tides") Katoppo was forced to step down as chief editor. I had just met Tides when the newspaper was closed and remember feeling sympathy and trepidation for him and his colleagues.

I was assigned as the U.S. Consulate Medan Public Affairs Officer in Medan from 1987-90. Information was scarce about conflict and suppression that occurred during those years. Only years later would these events become public knowledge. I heard some rumors about the February 1989 military attack against Javanese farmers at Talangsari, Lampung but I knew nothing of the full story. I also heard about a case of violence directed at the ethnic Chinese community in Medan but this was blacked out in the news. Soeharto kept sectarian violence under control in those days, but such violence occurred more often than I knew, and was kept under wraps.

In the late 1980s, the quiet, brave Legal Aid Foundation (Lembaga Bantuan Hukum, LBH) activist, Jafar Siddiq Hamzah, was monitoring human rights violations in Aceh and witnessed execution-style killings by the military. I lost track of Jafar after I left Medan. However, the next news of him I heard was a report in September 2000 that he had disappeared while visiting Medan in August and that he had been found murdered weeks later. His body was found mutilated in a forest 83 kilometers west of Medan, along with the bodies of several others.[118] He joined a very long list of Indonesian human rights activists who disappeared or were assassinated. Jafar would have completed his master's degree at The New School University (NSU) in New York had he not been executed. An NSU professor announced a scholarship in Jafar's name at a Jakarta conference in October 2000.

Another human rights martyr, Kontras Coordinator Munir Said Thalib, also spoke at that conference, calling for the murder to be investigated, just a few years before his own assassination. I can never forget the brutal assassination of Jafar, a sweet, thoughtful man who I knew personally.

In Medan in the 1980s, no one criticized the government except in very private locations and only in one-on-one conversations. Everyone assumed that if a second Indonesian was present, that person could be a spy, what in Aceh they called a *cunguk*. There was almost no political discourse and as a consequence, little political thought. Students were shy, even in university literature classes I taught.

Government servants supported Golkar, Soekarno nationalists supported the Indonesian Democratic Party (*Partai Demokrat Indonesia*, PDI), and devout Muslims supported the United Development Party (*Partai Persatuan Pembangunan*, PPP). Golkar always won by a landslide. Voting districts were so small that the government could track who voted against Golkar. Golkar's target was to win about 70 percent of the vote, enough to show overwhelming support but still show that people were free to vote for the other parties. Voting districts that voted against Golkar did not receive funding for government projects.

The Soeharto family monopolies over business made everyone discontented. No one could succeed in the private sector without the Soeharto family or their cronies wanting a piece of the action, or all the action, so entrepreneurs did not try very hard. Despite total government control over the media and free speech, foreign publications such as *The Asia Wall Street Journal* and *The Far East Economic Review* would publish articles revealing Soeharto's corruption. Government censors would blacken all negative news by pasting over parts of articles with black ink and paper, but it was easy to pull off the pasted paper and read the text. Copies of critical articles were distributed everywhere by fax. So, censored news got even wider attention and was spread by word of mouth.

It was obvious even in 1989 that Indonesia's economic prosperity and improved education system had already created the right conditions for democracy. I believed that democratic change would occur within a decade but I always assumed the transition would be violent. I witnessed the first signs of student democratic activism with the arrest of a student at the University of North Sumatra for speaking out politically, a very brave act at that time but a sign of the times.

In 1989, Indonesians assumed that Soeharto would step down very soon and allow free elections to choose a successor. However, when I asked well-educated people who they supported as the next president, the answer was almost always the same: the generals Benny Moerdani or Try Sutrisno, the two commanders of Indonesian armed forces during the 1980s, although Moerdani was also discounted because he was a Catholic. Sometimes B.J. Habibie was mentioned, the only civilian leader who people could envision as president, much admired for designing Indonesia's own passenger aircraft. Mostly though, people gave very little thought as to whom might replace Soeharto, probably assuming they did not have much choice in the matter.

The U.S. Embassy in the late 1980s promoted democracy and rule of law, but Soeharto's prickliness to criticism constrained us. We believed that direct criticism would be counter-productive. We could only point out Indonesian problems by referring to problems in the U.S., such as corruption, but the media were savvy enough to use those examples as oblique criticism of Indonesian government and smart readers got the point. We were very polite in what we said publicly but pushed quietly for economic and political reforms.

Paul Wolfowitz , who served as Ambassador from 1986-89, gave a controversial farewell speech at the end of his term, saying that greater openness was the key to economic success and that the same might be said for political success. This was the first speech by a foreign dignitary that criticized the Indonesian government and his speech was widely publicized and discussed.[119]

The U.S. Embassy was enthused about a fresh young face who burst onto the scene in 1987 when Megawati Soekarnoputri was elected to the Parliament (DPR). Soekarno's daughter was intelligent and engaging. We touted her potential to lead Indonesia someday. We even invited her to visit the U.S. on an International Visitors Leadership Program trip in 1989.

I left Indonesia during the 1990s to work in Malaysia and China, but happened to be visiting my wife's family in Jakarta in July 1996. I was walking around Menteng neighborhood when Megawati had rallied the PDI members and PDI youth barricaded themselves inside the PDI headquarters, the day before government troops broke up the rally. It really seemed at the time that democracy was gaining momentum.

I also clearly remember the year 1997 for Indonesia. All of my wife's relatives were becoming moderately successful in their businesses. Indonesia's economy was finally bringing prosperity to a burgeoning middle class. Then, late that year Asian monetary crisis (known in Indonesia as *Krismon*) hit and Henny's relatives were all financially ruined by the free falling rupiah and collapse of the banking system. It would take them a decade of hard work and sacrifice to recover but they did, and they are more prosperous today than they were in 1997.

In January 1998, international newspapers ran photos of a defeated looking Soeharto capitulating to the terms of the International Monetary Fund (IMF) bailout agreement, with IMF managing director Michel Camdessus glowering above him, symbolic of a subjugated king who has lost his mandate, his *mandala* (circle of spiritual power). The economic crisis, rampant corruption and immorality of Soeharto's family, as well as Soeharto's inability to control the May riots and massacres, sealed his fate. He had lost moral and spiritual authority to rule Indonesia.

Soeharto left power peacefully in 1998. For this, I will always admire him despite his cruelty. It was both exciting and amazing for me that Soeharto and his generals gave up power to the Indonesian people without bloodshed.

Today, most of my Indonesian friends and relatives are anti-Soeharto but some of them still love Soeharto. They tell me that Soeharto carried out successful economic and social policy until greed in his inner circle undermined his final years in power. I believe this is true but also believe that Indonesia's development as a democracy will far eclipse the performance under a patronage system where one man decided what was best for everyone. ❀

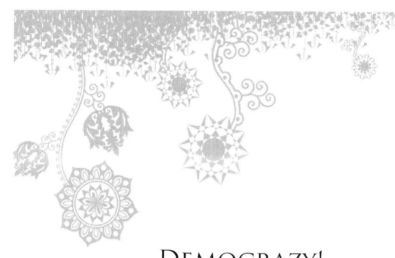

DEMOCRAZY!

So, when I returned to Indonesia in 2001, I was astounded with what Indonesians were calling "Democrazy" and I loved it. I even smiled at the crowds screaming "Satan" outside the U.S. Embassy, because this meant people were free to express themselves. During the decade I had left Indonesia, a nation of young activists led by veteran dissidents had slipped a Trojan Horse into the Hyatt roundabout (where many demonstrations gather) and out tumbled a raucous civil society.

While the generals were spying on activists, dissidents such as *Tempo Magazine's* founder Goenawan Mohamad were meeting out of sight at the *Utan Kayu*[120] artists community, secretly plotting how to bring about democracy, under the veil of poetry readings. The Institute for the Free Flow of Information (ISAI) and the Alliance of Independent Journalists (*AJI*) were building the foundation of a free press. NU's Gus Dur's and Muhammadiyah's Amien Rais were using their religious space to prepare their 70 million Muslim members to fight for democracy. At a time when the government apparatus was still using typewriters and sending faxes, democracy activists had mastered text messages and the Internet, with truth spreading across Indonesia like a bamboo forest in the rainy season.

This mousedeer (*kancil*) of a society I had known in 1989 burst out of the jungle as a young bull (*banteng*) in 1998. Pedicab (*becak*) drivers were elected to national Parliament. Former autocratic generals and the Soeharto regime's former thugs, *Pancasila* Youth, spouted the virtues of democracy. Democracy activists and radicals alike could not be silenced. I remember in the year 2000 staying in a home in Jakarta and hearing teenagers shouting nonsense all night over the nearby mosque's loudspeaker. No one had the authority to tell them to be quiet.

The national media emerged overnight as critical and mostly ethical. *Tempo Magazine's* talented young journalists exposed the economic crimes of billionaires. *Rakyat Merdeka* newspaper's outrageous and creative front page political cartoons poked fun of everyone, while its political muckrakers laid bare the corruption and sexual scandals of politicians. Even the conservative *Kompas* newspaper regularly published in-depth investigative reports and thorough news coverage rivalling *The New York Times*. *The Jakarta Post*, which I remember most in the 1980s for its strange but true stories that usually involved magical spirits, dedicated itself to publishing every story that was important for democratic *reformasi*, in clear, pungent English. Television stations also mushroomed, with an endless stream of political talk shows filled with heated debate and exposes on social problems. For example, I remember the *Kick Andy Show* interviewing parents who sold their 15-year-old girl into sexual slavery, alongside the girl and the pimp who trafficked her.

Journalists with all media faced threats, lawsuits and criminal prosecution but stood their ground.

In the U.S., Thomas Paine was the voice of freedom during the American Revolutionary War against England, but Indonesia has had a hundred such voices who put their lives on the line for freedom. I became close friends with most of them as the U.S. Embassy press attaché in 2001-2004. Indonesians should never forget that many journalists have been terrorized, beaten and killed over the years. AJI has an annual award for press freedom honoring one of Indonesia's journalist martyrs, Udin, believed to have been assassinated in 1996 in Yogyakarta, for reporting on alleged corruption involving a local official and Soeharto.

Similarly, countless human rights activists now with organizations such as the Commission for the Disappeared and Victims of Violence (Kontras),[121] the

Institute for Policy Research and Policy (Elsam),[122] DEMOS, the Human Rights Watch Coordinating Group (HRWG) and related organizations risked their lives under Soeharto. They continue to undergo great hardship to defend human rights, carrying on the torch of the great human rights martyr, Munir Said Thalib, who I will write more about later. I became close friends with these activists as the U.S. Embassy Democracy Unit chief from 2006-2009.

The father of Indonesia's human rights movement, Adnan Buyung Nasution, is a human rights lawyer of world standing who was imprisoned by both Soekarno and Soeharto for his activism. He guided the group of human rights leaders who drafted Indonesia's human rights laws and formed the Human Rights Commission (Komnas HAM), giving it real powers and moral authority to pursue past gross human rights abuses, even if political will to pursue these cases is still wanting.

The U.S. had its founding fathers, George Washington, Samuel Adams and Thomas Jefferson, to guide us through our fledgling democracy, but Indonesia had its democratic founding mothers and fathers facing just as monumental a challenge to achieve democracy.

The first *reformasi* president, B.J. Habibie (1998-1999), deserves credit for instituting a democratic constitution as his legacy when he could have turned the country over to another autocratic ruler. His sense of what was right for the country compelled him to rapidly institute many of the pillars of Indonesian democracy at its most fragile time.

President Abdurrahman Wahid (1999-2001), known affectionately as Gus Dur, strengthened human rights and pluralistic government in Indonesia, even for the long-oppressed ethnic Chinese community. He could have done so much more had he not suffered from ill health. Plus, he was funny, irreverent and beloved by all.

President Megawati Soekarnoputri (2001-2004) was a calming, staunch defender of democracy and nationalism during turbulent times, whose party also represented the aspirations of social justice. She had the strength to survive her father being taken away from her as a child and become a strong leader. Her love of gardening typified her dedication to the flowering of Indonesian democracy.

President Susilo Bambang Yudhoyono (2004-2014) brought strength, stability, anti-corruption and economic growth to Indonesia, despite his cautious style. He was a consensus maker determined to keep a pluralistic nation united. Under his watch, security sector reform went a long ways towards accountability, peace was achieved in Aceh and sectarian violence decreased everywhere.

Indonesia hopes that President Joko Widodo (2014) will bring a paradigm shift in the relationship between the people and its government, where government servants serve the people, not steal from them. He will be the first president to come from a humble background, outside the circle of the ruling elite.

In fact, each of the democratically chosen leaders were besieged by anti-democratic forces of the former autocratic regime, which never accepted defeat. These powerful and wealthy persons have plotted independently and in concert to undermine each presidency. Many of the major anti-government demonstrations, riots, sectarian violence and attacks on civil liberties have been organized and funded by anti-democratic forces.

Thankfully, each president was able to find the strength to defend democracy. In fact, the Government of Indonesia has become confident enough in its democratic institutions to take the lead in promoting democracy and human rights in Asia through the Bali Democracy Forum (BDF), initiated by President Yudhoyono and Foreign Minister Hassan Wirajuda in 2008. I accompanied U.S. Ambassador Cameron Hume to attend the inaugural forum and was surprised how Indonesians succeeded in gaining a consensus on several fundamental democratic goals from all the delegates, including from countries that were not democratic. The BDF might be called a vaccine against the "Clash of Civilizations" theory of Samuel Huntington. As President Yudhoyono said at the 2012 forum, democracy is rooted in Eastern, Western and Islamic culture.[123] ✿

Report the chicken missing, the goat also disappears[124]

"Come, sit, listen, be quiet, money," in Indonesian called the five "Ds."[125] Is there anyone who has lived in Indonesia who has not experienced the frustrating humiliation of being shaken down by public servants for bribes? For example, my Indonesian friends have had to pay extra fees for renewing their identification cards and driver licenses. Officials are most active in seeking extra money just before the end of fasting month, *Lebaran,* in order to fund their *Idul Fitri* celebrations.

The fact that the Anti-Corruption Commission (*Komisi Pemberantasan Korupsi,* KPK) has sent many ministers, governors, local regency heads (*bupati*), senior bureaucrats and parliamentarians to prison seems to have had little effect. I have personally known several politicians who went to prison and actually found myself feeling sorry for them as they seemed like such nice persons. Sometimes, these politicians know for certain that they will be caught by the KPK but still continue to give projects to cronies and accept kickbacks. They are shameless.

I do not have a scientific reason for this absurd behavior but I have a few theories:

- The Indonesian political campaign system requires large amounts of money to campaign and to buy votes, and voters expect gifts from all candidates.

- Most politicians have a weakness – sex, drugs, cars, wealth, etc.—and also have wives who want Gucci and Hermes bags and children who they want to send to the best schools.

- Politicians know the KPK will get them at some point for corruption that goes back many years. So, they believe they might as well make as much money as they can before going to prison.

- The amount of wealth acquired through corruption is easily worth a few years in a plush prison cell with a karaoke player, surrounded by friends and family.

- Politicians are not shamed by corruption and their friends do not seem to care either. They leave prison untainted by shame and flush with cash.

Unfortunately, voters have not been very wise in choosing members of national and local parliaments, but that is not really their fault. The Indonesian political party system makes it next to impossible for voters to elect effective lawmakers. Candidates run on the basis of buying votes through money and gifts. Many voters I have met have very vague concepts of what candidates stand for and participate in the process simply to get gifts from all the candidates.

Indonesia also has no campaign finance system so candidates go into debt to political patrons to raise money to campaign, and then pay back the patrons with spoils in the form of government contracts. Only a few politicians devote time or resources to helping their constituents.

Of course, the Dutch used corruption to divide and rule. Presidents Soekarno and Soeharto perfected the system. Under today's decentralization (*desentralisasi*), corruption has spread out of control everywhere. Businessmen say corruption is now worse than ever, requiring bribery at the local level from regents to governors, and all the way up to the national level. At least under Soeharto, businessmen paid 20 percent at the top and then could do business.

Furthermore, taxes are not collected so the government lacks revenue. Civil servants are paid low wages so bribery becomes a sort of tax to subsidize the salaries of civil servants, sometimes enough for them to buy Rolex watches and travel to Singapore on weekends.

The real victims are the vast majority of Indonesians who suffer from poor health care, bad roads, constant flooding of their homes, poor labor conditions and even being trafficked into human bondage, all because of pervasive corruption. Corruption in Indonesia breeds perpetual social injustice.

That is why many people hope Jokowi will be a revolutionary leader, changing perceptions of the people's relationship with leaders and what people expect. He realizes that corruption robs common people of social welfare. In Solo, by reducing corruption and maximizing public funds for the public good, his administration provided better health care, public services, infrastructure and a more prosperous life for everyone. However, at the time I wrote this, the Anti-Corruption Commission was under attack by institutions it is investigating. I can only hope that the President will act wisely and firmly to protect the KPK. I pray that anti-corruption and protection of human rights will be top priorities for the Jokowi government.

Corruption also exists in the U.S. but it does not cripple the social and political system as it does in Indonesia. When I was four years old, I got my first lesson in honesty. I saw a quarter on the ground and picked it up. My mother told me to put it back because it did not belong to me. I carried that simple lesson with me throughout life. When I was eight years old, our school class was taken to visit a prison to see how convicted felons live. A white collar criminal who had stolen from his company told us how he ended up in prison and his story frightened me. Even when our family was so poor and we did not have electricity or enough food, my father refused to accept help from the government, out of pride. In school, cheating on a test meant immediate expulsion from school and horrible shame. As a journalist and later as a civil servant, I knew that accepting gifts was a cause for being fired or imprisoned, and carried with it a stigma. Rejecting corruption is an attitude taught to Americans by parents and in schools, and is reinforced by peers throughout life. ✸

INVISIBLE TROOPS

When I think of gross human rights violations, accountability and impunity, I think of the term invisible troops (*pasukan siluman*), the rogue elements of the Indonesian military suspected to have instigated riots, and of kidnapping and killing civilians during the Soeharto era. Invisible troops also is a metaphor for the invisible nature of gross human rights violations in Indonesia going back decades. I have followed many of these cases over the years, knowing some of the victims (or their families) of kidnappings, torture, assassinations and massacres by security forces. Because I worked at the U.S. Embassy, I cannot write about these relationships or what people told me but almost everything I know has been published publicly in Indonesia, so I will write about what is publicly known.

There has been little accountability and almost complete impunity by Indonesian security forces. Cases brought to civilian courts almost always end up in acquittal. Cases brought forward by the Human Rights Commission (Komnas HAM) to the Attorney General Office (AGO) are kicked back to Komnas HAM for further investigation for procedural reasons. Meanwhile, Komnas HAM does not have the authority to formally investigate cases. Furthermore, the AGO will not investigate some cases that require an ad hoc court to pursue. The Parliament and the President will not establish these courts because the cases have not been officially investigated. This is a vicious circle.

While Komnas HAM has vigorously pursued all major human rights cases, political leaders lack the political will to take action needed to pursue these. Furthermore, many investigative reports are never made public. An important example was the national investigative team report, which was never released, that looked into the 1999-2002 religious sectarian violence in the Maluku Islands. This violence killed more than 5,000. Many people believe the violence involved members of the military and police. In cases tried in military courts, such as the 2007 case of marines who shot and killed farmers in East Java, the sentences were minor and senior officers were not held accountable.[126]

For details on these cases, the reader can refer to the annual U.S. Department of State Human Rights Reports or to the many reports by human rights groups such as Kontras and Indonesian Association of Families of the Disappeared (IKOHI). The below matrix from a 2011 Kontras report presents an overview of the results of major human rights cases.[127]

Convictions for Gross Human Rights Violations in Indonesian Human Rights Courts

Named in Komnas inquries	137
Indicted by AGO	34
Convicted at trial	18
Upheld on appeal	0

Number of major cases where known suspects were named in Komnas HAM inquiries: Tanjung Priok, Abepura, East Timor, and Trisakti I and II

A litmus case for accountability is the September 7, 2004, assassination of Munir Said Thalib, poisoned with arsenic on a Garuda Airlines flight to Amsterdam. Munir founded many of Indonesia's most important human rights organizations and human rights activists believe the motive for his murder was his investigation into major human rights cases. Human rights lawyers believe he was assassinated by security forces. For example, one theory is that he had discovered the role that members of security forces played in the disappearances of students in 1998 and the violence in East Timor in 1999.[128]

A 2004 fact-finding team ordered by presidential decree has never been made public but many of the details of the investigation have been reported by the media or brought to light during the trials against suspects in the murder. During the trials sessions I attended, I heard public testimony regarding how Munir suffered agonizing pain on the long Garuda flight, with stomach cramps and vomiting until he died during the flight. I heard alleged plots to assassinate Munir that involved a complex cast of characters from airline executives and a rock musician to a network of professional assassins, which prosecutors allege was planned by intelligence officials with motives of retaliation or repression. The case is shrouded in mystery.

The case did result in a degree of accountability in that a Garuda Airlines co-pilot, Pollycarpus Priyanto, was convicted of murder for having carried out the actual poisoning of Munir. However, he only served eight years of his 14-year sentence and was set free on parole in 2014 based on serving two thirds of his sentence. Indonesian human rights groups criticized the Jokowi government for paroling him and asked for the murder case to be reopened.[129] A more senior suspect was acquitted of charges.[130] That case largely fell apart due to the failure of key witnesses to appear.[131]

Munir left behind a widow, Suciwati, and two children. The stoic Suciwati is a former human rights labor lawyer who Munir once said was the braver of the couple. *Time Magazine* named her one of "Asia's Heroes" in 2005, by virtue of her keeping this case at the forefront of national and international attention, despite threats and the psychological drain of pursuing a case against such great odds of succeeding. I often saw her at diplomatic receptions, pressing ambassadors to speak out for justice in this case.

The Munir case is important both because it occurred after democratic *reformasi* and because it was the one case where the world held out hope of accountability. Indonesia has left countless victims of human rights abuses and their families without justice, truth or closure. There are untold victims of massacres in Indonesia buried in lost graves in the jungle or perhaps under some toll road in Jakarta. Their families are still waiting to bury their loved ones.

At the U.S. Department of State, there has historically been a debate on balancing past human rights abuses versus the reality that Indonesia is a young democracy that, since the year 2000, has made remarkable progress in addressing human rights issues. Human rights activists in Indonesia, in my experience, are also realistic and want to look forward, not backwards. However, continued transgressions of human rights for economic and political motives threaten democracy and harm people. Children are trafficked, farmers are kicked off their land, and prisoners are tortured. Anyone complicit in such crimes should be held accountable.

The world does not really forget atrocities. In fact, they remain ugly scars in the flesh of a nation until such time as society truly addresses them. The U.S., for example, has never truly made amends for the Sand Creek Massacre of 1864, where the U.S. army slaughtered over 100 Indians in my home state of Colorado, mostly women and children. This atrocity is mourned by the Arapahoe and Cheyenne tribes to this day in an annual commemoration held at Sand Creek.

The way the U.S. treated African Americans also is still a cancer for the U.S., a legacy of past injustices.

Many blacks feel alienated even after hundreds of years of living in America, despite notable progress in the past 50 years. The protests and riots by blacks in Ferguson, Missouri, in 2014 reflect the frustration of blacks across America. For example, blacks are 21 times more likely to be killed by police than are whites.[132] Hispanic Americans are also victims of many hate crimes, particularly by anti-immigration hate groups who profile Hispanic U.S. citizens as illegal immigrants. While President Obama has done much to address these injustices, minorities in the U.S. must still fight hard for their civil rights, be they Native Americans, blacks, Hispanics, Jews or Muslims.

Most shocking was the news in December 2014 of the horribly inhumane torture by the CIA of terrorist detainees, revealed by the U.S. Senate Intelligence Committee report. Fortunately, the Senate revealed the full extent of this torture as a deterrent to it ever happening again. However, there has been no accountability. For the sake of those victims of torture and for U.S. standing as a society which stands for human rights, it is crucial that the U.S. justice system bring those responsible to justice. Policymakers who ordered the tortures, and those who committed the tortures or were complicit, should be brought to justice. President Obama should take the lead in ensuring accountability. The world should never forget these acts of torture until there is justice.

Indonesia is a young democracy, and can do so much better than the U.S. in its first generation of striving to be a free and just society. Past human rights violations will never be forgotten. ✺

Human Slavery

From 2006-2009 I coordinated the U.S. Embassy Jakarta's efforts to combat Trafficking in Persons, investigating human trafficking and working with the Government of Indonesia on combatting this crime against humanity. I was very pleased when the anti-trafficking law of 2007 was passed, providing unparalleled protections for victims of trafficking. I also worked with Indonesian and international organizations that fought hard against wealthy and greedy people who would subject Indonesians to rape, torture and bondage for money.

During the years I investigated human trafficking in Indonesia, I learned that the process typically begins with someone's neighbor or uncle, who finds persons who need money and offers them a job. These victims are then sent to employment agencies in big cities, where they are imprisoned in fenced compounds before being sold to traffickers. They might be trafficked as maids, hotel workers, prostitutes, etc. across Indonesia, or sold abroad to places like Malaysia, Saudi Arabia and Iraq.

Here are a few of the stories I encountered:

In Manado, a mother told me about her 15-year-old daughter, a Minahasa girl from the hills outside of Manado in northern Sulawesi, who went to a remote city in Eastern Indonesia to live with her uncle. He promised her a good job and to pay for her education. On her first day in her new home, the uncle sold her into prostitution at a karaoke club. She refused, called home and tried to escape but was murdered before she could flee. The mother traveled to the city where her daughter was murdered but got no help from police. Later, the head of the anti-trafficking police unit from the girl's home province traveled to Eastern Indonesia with photos of all the young girls who had been trafficked there and rescued many.

I also heard the story of a 14-year-old girl from Bogor, West Java, who had just returned home, ruined for life. She had gone to Batam to work but was immediately enslaved, put into a tent near the port where she was raped 20 to 30 times a day. She lasted one month before she went insane. Traffickers gave her to a trucker to send her home and she was raped by trucker after trucker until she reached home.

I also visited the migrant workers terminal at Soekarno-Hatta Airport. On a random day, I met dozens of women who had been trafficked. In one room, a woman who had just gotten off the plane, crazed from being raped and beaten in Saudi Arabia, was chained to a bed to constrain her. I spoke to many trafficking victims on my visits to that terminal. I also met with women at employment agencies about to be sent to Saudi Arabia. I asked if they knew the risk of being trafficked. They all said yes, but that many also got good jobs, so they were willing to take the risk.

In Batam, Sumatra, I met with a large crowd of men just sent back from Malaysian migrant worker prisons. I asked them how many had been lashed in Malaysia as a punishment for being illegal migrant workers. All of the 100 or more men responded by pulling down their pants and showing me the fresh scars on their buttocks.

Trafficking has become more profitable than drugs, thus attracting many participants: employment agencies, ministry of labor officials, mafia bosses, police, military, and senior politicians.

Trafficking is also a large problem in the U.S., probably less known because it does not get much publicity. Based on public meetings on trafficking I have attended in Colorado, U.S., law enforcement agencies and social service organizations are working hard to stop human trafficking but human trafficking in the U.S. is still a major problem.

Anyone who uses prostitutes, works maids seven days a week for slave wages, or even buys products that were produced by slave labor is complicit in trafficking.

To end this chapter on an inspiring note, on the second day of Hari Raya (Idul Fitri celebrations after the fasting month) in 2007, as I celebrated at a relative's home in Bogor, my cell phone rang with a call from Kurdistan, Iraq. An Indonesian woman, Elly Anita, breathlessly told me how she had been lured there with a job offer as a secretary in Dubai but instead was trafficked to Kurdistan in 2006, where she was expected to work as a waitress. When she refused, the owner of an employment agency in Kurdistan put a gun to her head, beat her and starved her.

However, Elly got access to the Internet, contacted a friend, and got the phone numbers of the Indonesian Embassy in Amman, Migrant Care in Indonesia and, somehow, my cell phone number. It was not easy to get her out, but we stayed in constant contact with her and eventually she escaped at great risk with the help of International Organization for Migration (IOM), Migrant Care and the Indonesian Foreign Ministry. She now works for Migrant Care and has helped six other women trafficked to Iraq to escape. I nominated her as one the U.S. Department of State Trafficking in Persons Heroes in 2009 and she was one of just 10 chosen worldwide.

The three Indonesians I nominated as TIP Heroes during 2006-2009 were all selected as world heroes. The other two were: Wahyu Susilo, Founder and Director of Migrant Care, whose efforts have saved the lives of thousands of overseas migrant workers;

and Nirmala Bonat, a domestic worker in Malaysia who was beaten and burned with an iron. This young woman stayed in Malaysia for four years after barely escaping with her life from the home where she was trapped. Living at the Indonesian Embassy, she pursued justice in the Malaysian courts for her case despite being humiliated in court, an inspiration to overseas domestic workers everywhere. ❋

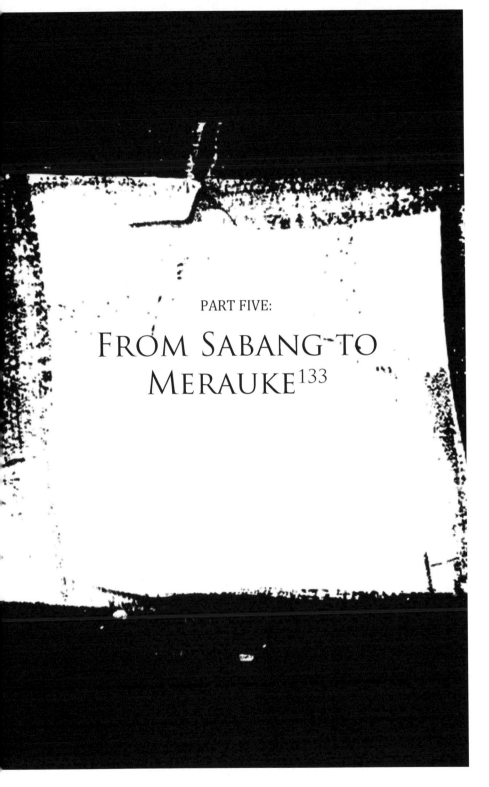

PART FIVE:

FROM SABANG TO MERAUKE[133]

VERANDA TO MECCA

The first time I visited Aceh in 1987, I was introduced
to the powerful Acehnese culture through its
dance. I saw a performance of the popular *Tari Saman*,
the "thousand hands dance." A mesmerizing rhythmic
chanting of verses from folk songs and the Koran,
the dancers moved their upper bodies and hands
in unison, building to a dizzying crescendo before
abruptly stopping and leaving the stage. I was left
breathless. The performance closed with a dance
which I was told was banned at the time and rarely
performed in public, the amazing *Rapai Daboh*. The
performer was a sheik with the title of *"Khalifah"* who
went into a trance while chanting verses to Allah,
pounding a sharp tipped *rencong* (dagger) into his

legs and then his abdomen with increasing force, until he was pounding with all his might. By putting all his faith in the all powerful Allah to protect him, the blade did not penetrate his flesh. I was told, however, that sometimes when faith is incomplete the performer could be badly wounded.[134]

To me, these dances represented the strong cultural identity that makes Aceh, as Indonesians like to describe the province, "special."

In 1987, the Indonesian government and Aceh were in a period of an uneasy lull in the civil war that began in the 1950s. The U.S. government was firm that Aceh is a part of Indonesia but urged the Indonesian government to take a humane approach to achieving peace. In addition, Aceh was economically important since Mobil Oil operated rich gas fields in Aceh with a field headquarters in Lhokseumawe, Aceh. USAID had large humanitarian assistance projects to improve the health of the impoverished, backward rural areas of Aceh.

At the U.S. Consulate in Medan, I focused on Aceh educational and cultural relations. USAID and the Fulbright Program had sent well over a hundred Acehnese scholars and civil servants to the U.S. for advanced degrees. This pool of talent was obvious in Aceh provincial government and at its premiere universities, Syiah Kuala University (Unsyiah) and the State Institute of Islamic Studies Ar-Raniry (IAIN Ar-Raniry), in the capital city of Banda Aceh.

Because of its scholar-leaders, Aceh was surprisingly well governed. Aceh had a tradition of Unsyiah rectors being selected as governors and of appointing university technocrats to government positions, different from other provinces where corrupt politicians and military officers got high positions. This system helped Aceh to develop economically and the central government to manage its Aceh problem through competent leadership. Later, Unsyiah scholars would play a major role in planning the reintegration of Aceh following the peace accord and in its reconstruction following the tsunami.

Despite the Indonesian government's efforts to build good schools, hospitals, roads and other infrastructure in Aceh in the 1980s, every single Acehnese I met in those years favored "Free Aceh," seceding from Indonesia. They viewed the Javanese and their culture as an imperialistic invasion. For example, I never wore batik shirts in Aceh, so popular everywhere else in Indonesia, because the Acehnese viewed batik as representing Javanese cultural imperialism.

The Acehnese wanted more economic benefits to flow back into Aceh from the wealth of natural resource revenues that flowed to Jakarta. They also wanted the military and police to stop using their power to steal from Acehnese citizens. In those days, the military budget was not sufficient to even feed its troops, so soldiers were encouraged to find ways to live off the local economy to survive, taking from the local citizens. The Free Aceh Movement (*Gerakan Aceh Merdeka*, GAM) fighters also stole from the people, who were exploited by both sides.

In traditional Acehnese attire during an Acehnese traditional ceremony in
Banda Aceh, approximately 1988.

Annisa Harsha, in
front, with three
Indonesian friends
in Banda Aceh,
February 2010, while
volunteering for
Banda Counseling
Center.

As importantly, the Acehnese wanted ownership of their culture, which is as deep and rich as those of the great kingdoms of Java and southern Sumatra. There is an old Acehnese saying, "When a child dies, you know where the grave is. When culture dies, where do you find the grave?"[135] For Acehnese, traditions are as important as wealth or power, and are synonymous with Islam, for reasons to be explained below.

Aceh is like an arm of Indonesia reaching out towards the Bay of Bengal, closer to Sri Lanka than it is to Java. During the age of trade and exploration, the prevailing trade winds connected Aceh trade with the Indian subcontinent and peninsular Southeast Asia, rather than with Java and the other archipelago islands. The Aceh Sultan wrote in a 1602 letter, "I am the reigning monarch who is below the winds, holding the throne of the kingdom of Aceh and Samudra, and of all the countries subject to Aceh, the lands below the winds."[136]

As the "Veranda to Mecca," a stopover for Southeast Asian pilgrims en route to the Haj in Mecca, Aceh became a melting pot and center of religious study for Indians, Persians, Arabs, Malays and Javanese scholars. Before Dutch colonialization, Aceh had diplomatic relations with Turkey, a trade agreement with England and interaction with the U.S., France, Portugal, China, and other countries as a sovereign state. Aceh's most famous leader, Iskandar Muda (1607-1636) brought Islam to the neighboring Gayo and Minangkabau regions. Javanese and Chinese immigrated to Aceh, as did the Minangkabau and Batak peoples from northern and western Sumatra. Today, the Acehnese are distinctive for their handsome blend of Indian, Arab, Malay and European (Portuguese) features.

Rich in pepper exported to the Red Sea, Aceh broke the Portuguese trade monopoly and even defeated the mighty Portuguese fleet at Bintan in 1614. Aceh and Siam were the only Southeast Asian nations that had never been subjugated by a colonial power, that is, until the Dutch invaded Aceh in 1893. The Dutch did not defeat the Aceh sultanate until 1904 and the Acehnese never fully surrendered, continuing their rebellion until the Dutch were driven out in 1942 by the Acehnese, the only part of Indonesia to expel the Dutch before the Japanese invaded.

Acehnese terrorized the Dutch with suicide attacks, armed with nothing more than the dagger-like *rencong*. Considered a sacred weapon with mystical power, the *rencong* is shaped like the Arab letter *bismillah*, and tucked into the front of the sarong. With its sharp tip and dull edges, it was designed to do only one thing, penetrate the abdomen when thrust within arm's length. Cut Nyak Dhien, Indonesia's legendary female war hero, used the *rencong* to kill the Dutch relentlessly in revenge for her husband's killing. She was not captured until she was old and almost blind, in 1901.

The Dutch regretted having ever invaded Aceh. During Holland's 40-year conflict in Aceh, it suffered the worst casualties and greatest loss of money of its 350-year colonial history.[137] The Acehnese suffered devastating losses as well. During the decade 1899-

1909 alone, four percent of Aceh's population was killed and perhaps 20 percent died, if diseases the Dutch spread are counted.[138]

The Indonesian government had just as a difficult a time managing what was called the "Aceh problem." In 1976, GAM leader, Hasan di Tiro, proclaimed Aceh's independence from Indonesia. In 1979, he went into exile in Sweden as the counter-insurgency campaign heated up. A decade later, in 1989, GAM operations rose again and Indonesian military operations in Aceh (*Daerah Operasi Militer or DOM*) intensified for the next nine years.

At the U.S. Consulate in Medan in the late 1980s, we could sense when the conflict got worse because of conflict along the road north from Medan to Banda Aceh. GAM would carry out attacks against buses carrying Javanese and the Indonesian military would respond by retaking the road and setting up military checkpoints. During those periods, we flew to Lhokseumawe and Banda Aceh for security reasons rather than taking the scenic two day car ride.

When I was assigned to Jakarta from 2001-2004, the war had again escalated. I was always worried about my friends in Aceh and sometimes they called me saying they were in danger of being killed. Both the military and GAM were capturing or killing civilians. Even neutral persons such as university professors were scared for their lives. In 2001, my friend Dayan Dawood, rector of Syiah Kuala University (Unsyiah), who was trying to broker peace between GAM rebels and the government, was shot dead, by one side

Dubes AS Tinjau Ruas Jalan USAID

BANDA ACEH (Waspada): Dubes Amerika Untuk Indonesia, Scot Marciel dalam kunjungan kerja ke Aceh meninjau pembangunan ruas jalan Banda Aceh - Calang, Selasa (11/1).

Scot dan stafnya dari Konjen AS Medan tiba pukul jam 09.00 Wib di jembatan Babahdua, Kecamatan Jaya Lamno, lantas memutar melintasi jembatan Kartika menuju ke Kawasan Gle U, untuk melihat proyek jalan.

Sekembali dari Gle U, Dubes menemui Camat Jaya, Idram SE. Dalam kesempatan itu Idram meminta Dubes mempercepat penyelesaian pembangunan Jalan yang sedang dikerjakan oleh USAID.

Idram dalam dialognya juga menyampaikan terimakasih kepada Rakyat Amerika atas bantuan untuk Aceh.

Harapan camat agar dilakukan percepatan pembangunan jalan itu ditanggapi Dubes dengan menyebut bahwa pembangunan jalan dan jembatan yang telah direncanakan itu merupakan prioritasnya. "Dubes juga menyampaikan akan membawa banyak investor agar putra putri Aceh bisa bekerja dan punya penghasilan untuk sejahtera," kata Idram kepada *Waspada*. Selain Camat, tampak Kapolres Aceh Jaya, AKBP Drs. Galih dan beberapa perangkat kecamatan dan desa di
· Kecamatan Jaya, kabupaten Aceh Jaya. *(b32)*

Waspada, January 12, 2011

U.S. Ambassador to Indonesia Scot Marciel, center, walking on a bridge at Babahdua in Lamno, Aceh, with me as U.S. Consul, January 12, 2011, when the United States was building a highway along Aceh's East coast as a contribution from the American people to the Acehnese people, following the December 26, 2004, tsunami.

or the other. Everyone was forced to take a side. Some Acehnese scholars fled to the U.S. to study on scholarships in those days with their families, just to escape the violence. It seemed that the conflict would go on interminably because too much blood had been spilled on both sides.

However, on December 26, 2004, the same Indian Ocean waters that had linked Aceh with Mecca brought a wall of water down on Aceh, killing 160,000 in Aceh alone and leaving a swathe of utter devastation. Many of my friends lived at the Unsyiah campus, which was located very close to the ocean, and was totally inundated. A professor there, who lost his wife and both his children to the tsunami which struck when he was away from home, told me that approximately 200 U.S.-educated teaching staff were killed. Another Unsyiah friend had a premonition of the disaster and took his family to higher land minutes before the 100-foot wave struck. Today, one can talk to almost anyone in Banda Aceh and learn that they lost most or all their family in the tsunami.

Soon after the tsunami, the U.S. State Department under the Bush-Clinton initiative provided 100 Fulbright scholarships to Aceh to help replenish the talent that was lost.

This devastation also destroyed the will of both the Acehnese and the Indonesian government to fight a civil war. The 2005 Helsinki Peace Agreement brought peace in rapid succession after the tsunami.

One of the GAM peace negotiators was in the Banda Aceh prison when the tsunami flood waters rose inside the prison that day. He fled to the second floor prayer room, punched his way to the roof and rode out the flood. This veterinarian and former rebel was elected the first governor of post-conflict Aceh. Intellectual and spirited, Governor Yusuf Irwandi was famous for driving himself around the province in his old Jeep Cherokee, chasing down poachers who violated his 2007 moratorium on logging.

The fiery Governor Irwandi courageously kept peace in an Aceh traumatized by decades of war, walking a tightrope between Indonesian government officials and military officers who believed that Aceh would return to its war of seccession, and former GAM members who indeed intended to pursue independence someday.

I witnessed this tension in 2009, when I traveled across Aceh as part of an international elections monitoring effort to help ensure peaceful elections, which I coordinated. The mere presence of international monitors helped to prevent some violence and this had a calming effect on a nervous electorate. Rumors were circulating like wildfire about agent provocateurs intending to instigate violence. The Aceh people, having lived through generations of violence, believed such rumors and panicked. In addition, robbery and other violent crime were high, committed by unemployed former combatants from both the GAM and the military (TNI), making people feel insecure. Thousands of former fighters, without a job or job skills, made the situation volatile.

I began my trip overland from Medan, travelling north up the east coast through Langsa, territory where the former GAM and its successor political party Partai Aceh (PA) had strong support. Along the east coast, former PA members talked proudly of the war for Aceh independence.

On the north coast approaching Banda Aceh, I headed into some of the most hotly contested territory of the civil war, the cities of Lhokseumawe, Bireuen, and Sigli. Talking to villagers, I heard tales of brutality committed by both the TNI and GAM during the long conflict and their ceaseless search for the hidden graves of their loved ones. An Aceh Truth and Reconciliation Commission and an Aceh Human Rights Court was supposed to have been set up under the Helsinki Accord but never materialized. Perhaps both former GAM members and the Indonesian government were not anxious to see what such a commission would uncover.

I then traveled along the West Coast Highway that USAID was building as a gift to the Aceh people, from Banda Aceh towards Meulaboh. The highway was beset by a host of issues: former PA members extorting money from the builders, Javanese workers being scared away by Acehnese, sabotage of newly built portions of the road and equipment, difficulty getting land rights from villagers, and monumental logistical challenges of carving through steep sandstone hills, bridging rivers and crossing mangrove swamps. The road was long overdue and way over budget, so the Acehnese were doubtful that the 144-kilometer road would ever be built. However, America keeps its promises. The road was opened in 2011, an engineering wonder that would allow fishermen and farmers along the impoverished west coast to get their products to market in Banda Aceh and beyond.

I also traveled to the Gayo highlands, to the major city of Takengon, the center of sectarian conflict between ethnic groups during the civil war. The local Gayo people and the impoverished Javanese farmers who were sent to this area by the Indonesian government as transmigrants to farm coffee had no cultural affinity with the coastal Acehnese, so sided with the Indonesian government during the conflict. The Gayo people, and TNI backed militias composed mainly of ethnic Javanese, supported breaking away from Aceh and forming new provinces: the Gayo and Aceh Leuser Utara provinces.

In a village south of Takengon, I talked to an old Javanese coffee farmer who had walked by foot into Aceh 47 years ago, cut away forest and planted coffee. He opposed GAM and PA as sources of conflict but also said the worst time was when the military came during the DOM years. The best times were now, he said, peaceful.

I talked with ex-GAM soldiers who felt left out from the peace dividend. They had turned in their guns for plows but could barely survive from the garden plots they were given. They resented that a few ex-GAM had gotten rich while most ex-combatants lived in poverty. Many ex-combatants and their children had not even attended grade school, so training them for jobs was difficult.

It was clear to me from this trip that Aceh still faced many years of painful rehabilitation from more than 30 years of conflict. After all, conflict caused 30,000 deaths, displaced 400,000 people and caused over $10 billion in damage. Thirty nine percent of Acehnese considered themselves victims of the conflict. The Reintegration Fund from the Aceh government helped ex-combatants and conflict-affected groups, providing villages across the conflict areas with improved welfare. Still, it will take years before the ravages of war can truly be repaired. The psychological scars may never heal.[139]

Aceh history turned another page in 2010 with the return of GAM founder Hasan di Tiro to Aceh, to reclaim his Indonesian citizenship and die in his homeland. That year I had a conversation with Hasan di Tiro's closest advisor, Zaini Abdullah, a thoughtful medical doctor. He emphasized getting more assistance to conflict victims (especially women), helping farmers and ensuring more transparency in government. He was elected governor in 2012, running with former GAM military commander Muzakir Manaf as the vice governor.

I also met several times with the soft spoken, charismatic Muzakir Manaf, whose low-key demeanor belied the fact he had commanded tens of thousands of fighters during the civil war. He told me that "we want to be one with Indonesia but Aceh has a specialness that has to be accommodated under the (Helsinki Accord)."

A myth about Aceh is that its people are fanatical Muslims, a misinterpretation of how the Acehnese see the world. A society based in the Malay world but historically oriented towards Mecca and the Ottoman Empire, Aceh developed a strong self-identity, committed to Islam but also to Acehnese custom, language and culture.[140] This syncretism of Islam, customs and sense of history is the only way to appreciate the Acehnese cosmic viewpoint.

Acehnese are conservative but also easy going. Having intimate relations out of wedlock definitely will be noticed and invite trouble. Liquor is found only at Western hotels. Foreigners are free to go about their ways in designated places: to drink beer in Western hotels and wear bikinis at the beautiful sands and coral reefs of Sabah island just off the Aceh north shore. Sabah feels a bit like Bali.

Many Acehnese are quite secular in their world viewpoint, particularly former GAM who spent years fighting a war. There was dissent in Aceh when the President Wahid government granted Aceh sharia law (Qanun Jinayat) for Muslims in Aceh in 2001, under pressure from the Ulama Consultative Council (MPU). Acehnese are devout so they readily accepted sharia law, but some maintain that it was not as high a priority as issues such as human rights or revenue sharing.[141] Today, some Acehnese do not like that sharia law is stigmatizing Acehnese as fanatical.

In any case, sharia law solved none of Aceh's most pressing issues. I read stories about its current excessive implementation, such as lashing unwed couples found together, outlawing women from wearing pants in some parts of Aceh, and imposing sharia for non-Muslims. Such practices do not strike me as very Acehnese. During my brief visit to Banda Aceh in November 2014, I saw no signs of sharia law being implemented against non-Muslims, who were still free to drink beer in Western hotels. I saw non-Muslim Indonesian women walking in public without a headcover. As usual, stories of fanaticism in Aceh are exaggerated in the media.

On the other hand, at a seminar I heard Acehnese women complain bitterly about cases of excessive implementation of sharia. One young female human rights activist told of a woman accused of khalwat (close proximity to the opposite sex) whose both legs were broken and her mother beaten.

Such laws are tainting Aceh as religiously fanatical, which it is not, and are scaring away tourists and investors. Aceh has some of Indonesia's most beautiful white beaches, pristine forests with orangutan and tigers, and an amazing culture of music and dance. Banda Aceh is a very clean, livable city with an airport that is an international gateway. What a shame if the Veranda to Mecca closes itself to the world with intolerant laws.

The Helsinki MoU provided that: "Kanun Aceh will be re-established for Aceh respecting the historical traditions and customs of the people of Aceh and reflecting contemporary legal requirements of Aceh." This provision was important for the Aceh people to protect their rich traditions but needs to be implemented wisely.

If I were to choose one custom which most epitomizes the Acehnese, I would say sipping coffee in coffeehouses. All day long, coffeehouses in Banda Aceh are full of men and women sharing stories or bargaining in politics and business. By 8 p.m., the women have gone home but the men, and a few wives, stay until at least 2 a.m. Acehnese know how to party, over a cup of coffee.

THIS IS MEDAN BRO!

"**B**rave, spirited, firm, no BS, so that they are proud to be a child (of Medan)," wrote Jaya Arjuna from North Sumatra University.[142]

Medan is truly the *gado-gado* (Indonesian mixed salad served with peanut sauce) of Indonesia—a delicious, exciting blend of many flavors competing for attention: Batak, Minangkabau, Malay, Acehnese, Javanese, Chinese, Sundanese and Tamil Indian plus smaller ethnic populations from Nias Island, Afghanistan, Pakistan, northern India and a few *bule* (Caucasians). I can think of nowhere else in Indonesia where one can find so much diversity and history within a 30-minute walk or so much anthropological and natural wonder within a few hours' drive.

In writing this chapter, I remember my late friend, historian Tengku Luckman Sinar,[143] who dedicated his life to documenting North Sumatra's past, as well as my friends from the Indonesian Heritage Trust, who have done so much to document and preserve Medan's priceless cultural heritage. Medan's historical buildings are threatened by economic development but are still better preserved than in other major Indonesian cities.

With the its cultural mélange of ethnic Bataks from the surrounding hills, Minang from West Sumatra, Acehnese from the north, Javanese (Deli), and coastal Malays, blended with influence from Portuguese, Dutch, Indian, and Arab cultures, Medan is "truly Asia."

One of my favorite Medan neighborhoods is Kampong Madras, where I often ate spicy Tamil Indian dishes in small restaurants. The Mariamman Hindu Temple was built in 1884 for the thousands of Tamils who came to work in the rubber and other plantation estates around Medan. The Sikh Gurdwara Sahib temple was built by Medan's prosperous Sikh population. Not far away is the Chinese Buddhist Shrine.

At the Maimun Palace, where Malay royalty still live and maintain the palace, the ancient grandeur of the Malay kings is evident. I recall nights sitting on a straw matt listening to an old Melayu (Malay) man compete with an old woman in *pantun*, the 15th century Melayu tradition of trading poetic jibes. At Medan poetry readings I attended, I heard readings from the great "son of Medan" Chairil Anwar (1922-1949), who created Indonesia's most loved poetry during his short life.

The heart of historic Medan (Medan was named by a Turkish admiral from the word *"Medina"* or town) is *Lapangan Merdeka* (Freedom Square). Near this central plaza are many well preserved 19th century buildings, including the lovely London Sumatra building. From there, one can wander among the charming old Chinese shophouses of Kesawan.

I often visited one of Southeast Asia's most important monuments to Chinese history, the ancestral home of Tjong A Fie, now a museum run by his descendants. My friend, Fon Prawira Tjong, dedicated his life to preserving the home as an historical monument. Fon died in 2014 but his work will be carried on by his family. The U.S. Ambassador's Fund for Cultural Preservation gave a large grant to help restore part of the mansion in 2014, fulfilling one of Fon's dreams before he died.

Tjong A Fie was the community leader of all the Chinese workers and merchants the Dutch brought to North Sumatra. He built bridges, hospitals and schools that still stand today, and donated to Medan its famous old Clock Tower. Today, Medan's population is 20 percent ethnic Chinese.

Adventure awaits in all directions from Medan. In the fertile Deli valley are palm oil, rubber and tobacco plantations, planted in the 1870s when immigrants from China, Java, India and surrounding areas came to northern Sumatra for work. In the 1980s, I often visited the American Goodyear plantation, where Americans lived and schooled their children at home. By the stroke of dawn, Tamil tappers had extracted the valuable

A traditional pantun poetry recital ceremony in North Sumatra that I attended in approximately 1989.

rubber, exactly the way it was done a hundred years ago.

Today, however, palm oil is king. I can drive for days on end through Sumatra's palm oil plantations from north to south. Palm oil is more valuable than oil and an important source of revenue. However, the forests are being decimated to cultivate palm oil, which is environmentally unsustainable. It is too late to restore the forests but Indonesia cannot afford to lose more of its forest cover, which can only be saved if Indonesia enforces its forestry laws. In North Sumatra, one important solution is to teach communities how to use the jungles for ecotourism, taking advantage of the valuable jungle ecosystem.

A short drive from Medan is the Mount Leuser National Park, where tigers, orangutans, rhinos and other rare, endangered species are losing the battle against deforestation of their habitat. At Bukit Lawang, a couple of hours drive from Medan, guides take tourists to see the 8 a.m. feeding of milk and bananas to the orangutan, which are being rehabilitated to return to the wild. During hikes deeper into the jungle, I twice encountered the orangutan queen of the park, Mina, who blocked the trail demanding rambutan fruit as a bribe to pass. Of course, Mina is only trying to adapt to a habitat encroached on by palm oil plantations, where she cannot find enough fruit in the wild to survive. One very promising effort to protect the North Sumatran rainforest and conserve the natural habitat is that of Dr. Ian Singleton, whose Sumatran Orangutan Conservation Programme works to rehabilitate formerly captured orangutan in a way that is sustainable. His project is raising public awareness of the importance of saving Southeast Asia's only great ape and conserving its forests, in the face of short-sighted economic pressures to deplete the forests.

Mount Leuser National Park is one of the most diverse tropical forests in the world, valued at $400 million in economic return if preserved, with potential for its medicinal wealth, sustainable jungle agriculture and ecotourism. It is the only park where orangutans, tigers, rhinos and elephants can all be found in the same jungle. On longer guided treks into the park, endangered tigers are sometimes spotted. My old friend, New Zealand ecologist Mike Griffiths, has dedicated his life to preserving Mount Leuser. He has captured on camera its many amazing species: clouded leopard, mousedeer, python, siamang, macaque, leaf monkey, sun bear and the golden cat, to name a few.

A short drive from Bukit Lawang is Tangkahan, where tourists can ride elephants on a jungle trek, an exhilarating experience as the massive animals carry passengers up and down steep, muddy trails choosing each step carefully and gently. Before the trek begins, tourists are asked to first help scrub elephants with brushes in the river, which the elephants love. Former wildlife poachers now work as tour guides and as jungle scouts, protecting the wildlife they used to hunt, and learning to plant sustainable jungle crops, such as wild durian.

In the interior of North Sumatra are the Batak tribes: Karo, Toba, Pakpak, Simalungun, Angkola, Mendailing, Alas, Kluet, and Singkil, each with their own ancient traditions. The first historical mention of the Bataks was by the ancient fifth century BC Greek historian Herodotus.[144] In 1292, Marco Polo lived among what he termed the "wild" Batak. Legend has it that the first Christian Missionary to not be eaten by the Bataks was the German Lutheran preacher Dr. Ludwig Nommensen, who in the 1880s used his empathy with Batak culture to convert them. The Batak Christian Protestant Church (HKBP) was founded in Balige, North Sumatra in 1917.

North Sumatrans say that one Batak will sing and play the guitar, two will play chess and three gathered together will form a choir. On Sunday mornings at Lake Toba, I enjoyed the beautiful Batak church choir voices booming from churches which surround the volcanic hills around Lake Toba. In the middle of Lake Toba is the small Samosir Island, a tranquil and unspoiled place filled with art and song. I used to stay in one of the many charming lakeside cottages and walk from village to village, viewing wooden carvings that represent ancient spiritual practices.

Near Lake Toba live the Karo Batak, who farm vegetables beneath the smoldering and often erupting Mount Sinabung and Sibayak volcanoes. In September

Children at a camp in Berastagi, North Sumatra, displaced from their homes beneath the erupting Sinabung volcano, are in good spirits in September 2010 during a visit.

2010, I was in Medan when Sinabung spewed fire and ashes 5,000 meters into the air, and walked on the thick ashes to visit the 17,000 refugees that farmed near the mountain. At this writing, it has erupted for the third time in the past four years.

Visiting Nias Island in North Sumatra is like stepping back into a Stone Age culture. In South Nias, one can visit villages where young men still leap over two meter tall stone towers as a rite of passage. My friend, the Reverend Lase, broke both his legs in this ritual. The Nias economy and social system are centered around pigs. All wealth, including the value of a bride, is measured in pigs. Off the south coast of Nias are world class surfing sites packed with surfing vagabonds. Nias culture is ancient, unique and hidden, among the most intriguing places in Indonesia. ✿

EARTH GODDESS

When I am on the road in Indonesia and hungry,
I eat *Nasi Padang*, the West Sumatran spicy
smorgasbord of foods piled on my table like a feast.
Only Minang food can be found in every little village
across Indonesia. I could eat *Nasi Padang* every day of
the week and never get tired of it.

My memories of West Sumatra go back to the
1980s, when Padang was a sleepy city where I
would hire a one-horse *bendi* cart instead of a taxi.
Even under the repressive Soeharto regime, Minang
intellectuals spoke of their desire for democracy and
free speech. Islam in this Muhammadiyah stronghold
promoted a free thinking, entrepreneurial attitude.
While Minang Muslims are conservative, I never felt
religious intolerance, just a strong identity with the
homogenous Minang culture.

By 2009, West Sumatra had not changed much culturally but it had been discovered by tourists, so its economy was booming. Its lakes, beautiful islands, coral reefs and world class surfing had become internationally famous. A large number of Americans and Australians had settled in the capital of Padang to take tourists surfing.

Then, at 5:16 p.m. on September 30, 2009, a tremendous earthquake of 7.9 magnitude took place just 28 kilometers off the coast of West Sumatra's capital city of Padang. Over a thousand were killed and a quarter million people displaced. I arrived the next day in Padang to a scene of unimaginable destruction, to coordinate U.S. emergency response efforts. Padang was not recognizable and the countryside was hit even worse. International assistance flowed immediately into West Sumatra, including U.S. Navy ships which built a field hospital in Padang. U.S. navy helicopters

Delivering emergency assistance by U.S. Navy helicopter to an isolated village in West Sumatra devastated by the September 30, 2009 earthquake.

A year after the West Sumatra earthquake, visiting an elementary school in Padang which received assistance from USAID.

also flew emergency supplies to villages so isolated that it would have taken weeks for them to be reached by road.

I learned two important lessons from this experience about the Indonesian custom of *gotong royong* (community mutual assistance) and resilience. Success in the immediate rescue of victims and getting help to survivors was due to the ability of the Indonesian government and the West Sumatran provincial government to accept and manage massive international assistance. This calm management of thousands of outsiders was a monumental task amidst the dust and rubble of a cataclysmic disaster. Just two months later, when I celebrated the U.S. holiday of Thanksgiving with friends in Padang, I saw that West

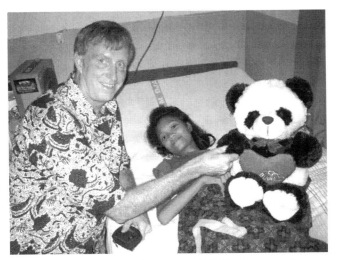

Bringing a teddy bear to Lani, badly hurt in the 2009 West Sumatra earthquake, at a Padang hospital.

Sumatra was already well on the way to recovery. A year later, when I attended the one year anniversary ceremony of the tragedy, I witnessed that the province had recovered physically, with important buildings such as schools rebuilt and markets bustling with trade. Of course, the tears were still flowing, and people were traumatized, fearful that disaster might strike again.

The Minang people recovered quickly from the earthquake because they depended mostly on each other to survive and thrive. A couple of weeks after the earthquake, I visited a little girl in the hospital, Lani, who was crippled from injuries suffered in the earthquake. She had a big smile on her face and was determined to go back to school and become another great Minang leader someday. She wanted to be President. She epitomized the Minang spirit.

The scrappy spirit of the Minang people can also be found in the story of their name. There is a story in the Minangkabau culture of West Sumatra about a contest between a Javanese bull with a local Minangkabau calf. The Minangkabau mounted spears on the calf's head in place of horns and starved it for three days before the contest. On the day of the contest, the calf saw the bull and ran to it to find milk, and in its thirst thrust the swords into the mighty bull's belly, killing it, thus winning the battle for the Minangkabau against the Javanese attackers.[145] This story symbolizes the independent nature of the Minangkabau people.

With a tradition of consensus building (*musya-warah*) and democratic election of local leaders (*walinagari*), who must leave office if they do not lead well, West Sumatra culture helped influence the democratic culture that was first planted in Indonesia in the 1950s. The egalitarian and transparent nature of Minang culture continues to play a role in national politics today, with a large number of Minang who are leaders in democracy and human rights.

The Minangkabau are a matrilineal society. Communal wealth is kept by the women, bringing stability and social welfare to the society. In fact, the origin mythology of the Minang is that they are descended from a queen, *Bundo Kanduang* (Earth Goddess), who from her home in Pagarruyung in Minangkabau, created the universe.[146] Minang women are strong, play an equal role in society and value education.

West Sumatra does not have many natural resources other than its green mountains, pristine lakes and blue ocean. Its farmers work hard to grow enough rice and vegetables to be prosperous. The men have few career opportunities in West Sumatra and cannot inherit wealth, so they migrate (*merantau)* to other parts of Indonesia seeking success, and they share their wealth with the people in West Sumatra. Thus, there are many national leaders from West Sumatra in all fields. In 2010, I attended the annual ceremony in West Sumatra where the Minang honor the native sons who migrated and repaid their success to the Minangkabau. That year, my friend Irman Gusman was given a title of local nobility for his success as the Chairman of the Indonesian Senate.

There is not space in this book to write about the rest of Sumatra. However, I have spent much time exploring Sumatra and will never exhaust all the adventures to be found there—from the lovely city of Pekanbaru, to the jungles and beaches of southern Sumatra. One of my favorite destinations is South Sumatra, where lies the ancient ruins of the Sriwijaya empire, Indonesia's great commercial kingdom that thrived throughout Southeast Asia from the 8th to the 13th centuries. The kingdom centered on the Musi River, which flows through the heart of the vibrant capital city of Palembang. South Sumatra is an example of a rich, well managed province under the leadership of Governor Alex Noerdin, who has brought thriving world trade to the province, in the tradition of Sriwijaya.

Before I leave Sumatra, however, I must pay tribute to my tough skinned friend, Andalas, a Sumatran rhino born in captivity in the Cincinnati zoo in 2001, who came back to his homeland in 2007, with the hope of adding diversity to the shrinking Sumatran rhino gene pool. Sumatran rhinos are shy, solitary creatures, so finding chemistry with the right mate is difficult. I met Andalas close up in the Way Kambas National Park in Lampung in 2010. I am pleased to announce that Andalas successfully bred with his mate Ratu. Their calf, Andatu was born on June 23, 2012, the first Sumatran rhino born at the Sumatra Rhino Sanctuary. Hooray for American-Indonesian matches! ✺

PAPUA

From Sumatra to the western border of Indonesia, a distance of 4,000 kilometers (2,500 miles), lies Papua. Even in a nation of exotic diversity, Papua stands out for its spectacular culture. My short visit to Papua was one of the most unforgettable trips of my life. On April 16, 2002, I landed in a small plane in the sleepy capital of Jayapura, accompanying U.S. Ambassador Ralph Boyce on the first visit by a senior U.S. official to Papua in many years. We were greeted at the door of the airplane by hundreds of Papuans dressed in traditional costume and jumping up and down in dance, chanting loudly. Dozens of the men wore only long penis sheaths and feathered headdresses, carrying spears. We were told that this was a traditional greeting ceremony and that we would walk to a nearby park for a cultural event. I thought it strange that government officials in their civil servant uniforms sat watching and did not meet us. Several grimaced and rubbed their foreheads.

As we walked in a parade, surrounded by naked men with spears who said they would act as our bodyguards, I could see that the U.S. Embassy security officer protecting the Ambassador was nervous. I knew that we had been hijacked on arrival by a delegation of self-determination activists when I heard loud chants of *"Papua Merdeka"* (Free Papua) and saw banners with the words in English, "WE ALL WEST PAPONENS (sic) ASK FULL INDEPENDENCE." I felt at that moment, as Indonesians say, "Like a chicken that sees a civet cat."[147] The parade finished at the grave of Theys Eluay, a martyr who had been killed the previous October. Ambassador Boyce was asked to put a bouquet of flowers on the grave. He had no choice but to comply reluctantly, surrounded by thousands of excited Papuans.

However, this gesture was seen by the Indonesian government as a sign of U.S. support for Papuan independence. The Ambassador's first meeting was with the upset Irian Jaya Governor Jaap Solossa (Papua was called Irian Jaya at that time). Sitting next to the Governor was Irian Jaya Police Chief General I Made Pastika, who later would gain world respect for his success as chief investigator into the Bali bombings, and is now the Governor of Bali. I whispered to Pastika that the best way to solve the misperception caused by the welcoming parade was for the Ambassador and the Governor to make an immediate joint statement to the media clarifying the U.S. policy position regarding Papua. In his statement, Boyce stated that the U.S. does not support separatist movements in Papua and did not appreciate being hijacked on arrival, and this was reported in all the media the next day, calming the situation.

Formerly Dutch New Guinea until being transferred to Indonesian administration by the United Nations in 1963, Papua is an extreme example of the difficulty Indonesia faces in maintaining national unity. The Austronesian Papuan language has no relation to the Indonesian language and the Papuan culture bears little resemblance to the dominant Javanese culture. Historically, the Javanese have mistreated the Papuans although that has improved since 2001 under *reformasi*.

President Jokowi has demonstrated that he cares about the problems of the Papuan people by visiting Papua twice during his presidential campaign and delivering a speech in Jayapura during Indonesia's national Christmas celebration in December 2014, soon after taking office. He pledged infrastructure development and an open dialogue, which are significant promises. Jokowi has proven that he takes a humanitarian approach to governing, which is also promising for Papuans.

An archipelagic country as diverse as Indonesia, with over 300 ethnic groups, constantly faces centrifugal momentum of separatist movements across the country. However, each island and every ethnic group are much better off as part of a strong, free and democratic Indonesia. The alternative would be chaotic and violent.

In the U.S., the federal system of government has worked brilliantly at keeping the nation peacefully united through respect by the central government for the rights of each of the 50 states. Nevertheless, there has been conflict between the states and the federal government. For example, when some states in the southern U.S. violated the civil rights of blacks in the 1960s, Washington, D.C. forcefully intervened to protect the rights of black citizens. To the extent that the Indonesian government defends the civil rights of all its citizens, Indonesia will be a stronger and more unified nation. ✸

TIMOR-LESTE

When I arrived in Timor-Leste in February 2007 as the interim chargé d'affaires to manage the U.S. Mission in Dili for a couple of months until the new ambassador arrived, I had the opportunity to witness an impoverished and destroyed nation struggling to rebuild and govern itself. Most startling was the aftermath of the 1999 scorched earth withdrawal of Indonesian troops from East Timor, in which the Indonesian military and pro-Indonesian militia utterly destroyed over half the country. Traveling from Dili westward towards Indonesia, I witnessed burned out buildings everywhere. Yet from Dili traveling east, the opposite direction of the Indonesian withdrawal, buildings were still intact, a postcard picture of a pastoral countryside with charming Portuguese-like seaside towns.

Timor-Leste's verdant mountains, white beaches and coral reefs are stunning. The Timorese-Portuguese-Indonesian cultural blend is fascinating. The people of Timor-Leste are kind and welcoming. Timor-Leste is a country which everyone falls in love with from the first day they arrive.

However, I was in Timor-Leste during some of its most turbulent months. Today, I have read that it is a much safer destination. International peacekeepers were able to leave in 2012.

In 2007, Timor-Leste's refugee camps were filled with internally displaced persons, leaving their homes to stay in the camps mainly to ensure personal safety and food security. Most people were in constant fear that rice would not last long enough to tide them through the upcoming "hungry" months, the period before the next rice harvest. Famine was a constant fear.

Most of the Timor-Leste's property records were burned during the fires set by the Indonesian security forces during their withdrawal, so many Timorese had no title to their lands. Indonesians had also bought up large tracts of prime real estate before East Timor achieved independence, so some land titles were held in Jakarta. Thus, many persons were displaced because of confusion over land rights. Gangs or militias tied to different political groups, calling themselves "martial arts groups," also terrorized the population, oftentimes kicking people out of their homes. Some militias were a legacy of Indonesian rule while others formed in recent years.[148]

When I was there, unemployed Timorese men would begin drinking heavily towards the end of the week so that the only safe days of the weeks to move around Dili were Monday and Tuesday. By Friday morning, discouraged and intoxicated men were attacking anyone with the only weapons they had, rocks or slingshots that shot lethal small arrows.

Most Indonesians resent that their country was not recognized by the international community for all it contributed to East Timor during the 25 years that it ruled the province. After all, when Portugal Timor declared its independence on November 28, 1975, after 400 years of colonial rule, Portugal had contributed next to nothing to the Timorese. Timor was used chiefly as a penal colony for political and criminal prisoners. Timorese were poor and uneducated.

The predominant political party advocating Timor independence, Fretilin, was seen by Indonesia, Australia and the U.S. as Marxist, at a time when Indochina was falling to communists and the communist "domino effect" was seen by the U.S. and Indonesia as a genuine threat.

The day before Indonesia invaded East Timor on December 7, 1975, in Operation Komodo, President Soeharto briefed U.S. President Gerald Ford and his aid Henry Kissinger on plans for Indonesia to invade Timor. The Americans gave tacit agreement, asking only that the invasion be "fast" and be delayed by a day until they left Indonesian airspace.[149] Another concern was that Indonesia had used American military equipment in the invasion.

By 1980, Indonesian rule in East Timor had left between 100,000 and 230,000 dead from military action, starvation or disease.[150] The most notorious human rights violation was the 1991 Santa Cruz massacre where Indonesian security forces killed 271 East Timorese during a pro-independence demonstration with as many more citizens disappearing and believed dead.[151]

The August 30, 1999, referendum in East Timor resulted in a vote for independence. More than 1,300 people were killed and hundreds of thousands were displaced during the violence that followed the vote.[152] The Indonesian Human Rights Commission (Komnas HAM) established the Commission for Inquiry for Human Rights Violations in East Timor to probe that violence, a credible investigation that was the basis for the binational Commission of Truth and Friendship (CTF) process by Indonesia and Timor-Leste, which issued its report in 2008.

I followed the final part of the CTF process closely and attended some of the public hearings. Notably, the final report rejected the idea of amnesty or political rehabilitation for individuals the Commission found guilty of crimes against humanity. This was because the worst perpetrators did not "cooperate fully in the disclosure of the truth."[153] The CTF brought to light crimes committed on both sides of the conflict.

Importantly for Indonesia, the CTF report arrived at some politically difficult findings. On one important point that many thought the CTF would sidestep, the report found that Indonesian-backed militias committed crimes of murder, rape, torture, and other crimes targeting supporters of independence. Most significantly, the report noted systematic institutional support for militia groups by the Indonesian government, including the army (TNI), police, and civilian government, through supply of money, food and weapons.[154]

For Indonesia, it is crucial that the CTF recommendations be implemented to prevent future such atrocities and impunity, such as the recommendation to: "Develop and implement a security reform programme aimed at enhancing the professionalism of security actors, establishing legal boundaries between civil authorities and the military and police forces..." In other words, CTF called for civilian authority over security forces and clear delineation of military responsibility for national defense as opposed to police authority for domestic security.

Poor governance and gross human rights violations undermined much of what Indonesia accomplished in East Timor during 25 years of rule. The destruction wrought in 1999 was shameful. However, the Timorese people were ready to forgive and move forward to build good relations with Indonesia. Importantly, the CTF process paved the way for normal and constructive relations between these two close brothers, Indonesia and Timor-Leste, with healthy trade, cultural exchanges and educational exchanges. Timor-Leste and Indonesia need each other as good partners. ✽

EPILOGUE

As I finish writing this book in February 2015, watching deer graze and snow fall softly outside my home in Colorado, I am anticipating my return to Indonesia next month, to its ubiquitous smiles, piquant scents of spices and chili peppers, and all of its surprises.

There are layers upon layers of complexities to unveil so that we can learn to respect each other: Indonesians and Americans; Muslims, Christians and Jews; liberals and conservatives.

If this book inspires a few Indonesians and Americans to learn more about a neighbor's religion, to demonstrate more tolerance for other beliefs and to speak out against religious bigots who are instigating hatred and conflict, then I am thankful. I also hope that this book conveys the message that Americans are overwhelmingly tolerant of all beliefs and respectful of Islam.

For the minority of Americans who fear Islam, Indonesians can help to enlighten them with how friendly and peaceful Indonesians are. When Indonesians come to the U.S., they should tell Americans about Indonesian democracy, freedom, and religious tolerance.

Also, Indonesians should make an effort to understand Judaism. Indonesians can help the Palestinians best by opening up dialogues with Jews.

I believe that religious intolerance is getting worse in both the U.S. and Indonesia. I find this frightening because religious intolerance leads to intimidation, violence and war.

Another important message this book has for Indonesians is the importance of fighting corruption, of having a mindset of honesty in government.

Human rights violations have caused Indonesians much suffering. The situation is much better since 2000 but still not perfect. Holding people accountable for human rights violations is very important for the welfare of Indonesian society.

I make no secret in this book about the hope that I place in our two presidents, Obama and Jokowi, to address the issues I raised. The world is fortunate to have such leaders. Because I got to know Jokowi during his first term as mayor of Solo and believe him to be an honest, humanitarian and smart leader, I believe he can lead Indonesia into an era of greatness. Indonesia can become a fair, just and prosperous nation in the next decade. On the other hand, I have observed the political challenges President Jokowi has faced during his first three months in office, so my hope has turned to cautious optimism. I will watch this new *wayang* play with fascination to see how Yudhisthira deals with adversity.

My stories about Indonesian culture tell Indonesians how I assimilated into their way of life and fell in love with Indonesia's richness and beauty. However, I also tried to write in a way so that Americans would gain some insight into Indonesia and want to explore it further. Once Americans visit Indonesia they fall in love with the people's kindness.

The global war against terrorism has been important in stopping hundreds or thousands of terrorists from repeating attacks such as 9/11 and the Bali bombing. Law enforcement in the U.S. and Indonesia has been tough and effective. Indonesia has also been very effective in reaching out to radicals to teach them moderation and to convert the minds of imprisoned terrorists from hatred to peace.

However, some past U.S. actions in the war against terrorism have made the situation worse, such as the invasion of Iraq and torture of terrorism suspects. An atmosphere of Islamophobia has isolated Muslims instead of reaching out to them. Obama has begun to change this approach to one that is more humanitarian. Americans should stand up for the rights of Muslim Americans the same way we have for the rights of blacks, Jews and other minorities who are treated unfairly.

My hope is that this book will contribute to understanding between religions and between the peoples of Indonesia and the U.S., and promote further dialogue. ❀

ENDNOTES

1. Indonesian: *Seperti bulan dan matahari,* a phrase describing a perfect match.
2. *Kejatuhan durian runtuh,* meaning, struck by dumb luck.
3. Padang food, spicy dishes from West Sumatra.
4. *Bule* is a slang word for Caucasian with a neutral connotation.
5. Noeke Ratna Padmiandari Mangoendipoero's blog: noekemangoendiepoero.wordpress.com. Mbak Noeke's writings on Javanese philosophy are based on family wisdom passed down generation to generation from the Majapahit Empire, including the books by her great grandfather, the philosopher Ki Padmosusastro. A sociologist, her analysis is written in her unpublished manuscript, *Tarian Dalam Diam (Dancing in Stillness: The Beauty of Javanese Ethics).* Her blog has excerpts from this manuscript. Her writings are based on both research and family lore, which she refers to as *Nir Aksara,* the unspoken and unwritten tradition. Javanese understand this philosophy but find it difficult to explain.
6. A current example of government leaders facing retaliation for enforcing honest behavior was reported in the December 31, 2014 *Kompas* newspaper in Jakarta, how previous Jakarta Governor Jokowi and his deputy Basuki "Ahok" Tjahaja were harassed by staff when they first took office, including destruction of Jokowi's chair and desk and turning off Ahok's electricity, Ahok told *Kompas.*

7. Suwardi Endraswara, *Falsafah Hidup Jawa,* Cakrawala, 2003.

8. *Ibu* means mother in Indonesian, a term used to respect any woman who is older than oneself, whether or not she is married or a mother.

9. An American friend of ours married to an Indonesian was once hypnotized by a friend and disappeared for a week while her family looked everywhere for her. When she finally broke out of the hypnotic trance a week later, she found herself alone in a small hotel in the mountains of Sumatra far from home, with no memory of how she got there. She only remembered being with the woman who hypnotized her a week earlier.

10. Arabic name for Jesus in the Koran.

11. I was raised in the Divine Science Church, which follows the teachings of Jesus as one of the divinely illuminated prophets but which also believes that other monotheistic religions, including Islam, reveal divine truth.

12. Naomi Schaefer Riley, "Interfaith Unions: A Mixed Blessing," The New York Times," April 5, 2013. Survey based on research conducted by Riley, author of, *Til Faith Do Us Part: How Interfaith Marriage is Transforming America.*

13. The United States Census Bureau, census.gov., "2010 Census Shows Interracial and Interethnic Married Couples Grew by 28 Percent Over Decade," April 25, 2012.

14. Padmo Ali, "Ki Padmosusastro Dan Karya-Karyanya," Sarong-Kalong.blogspot.com, May 6, 2012.

15. In Javanese, *"Tiyang mardika ingkang marsudi Kasusastran Jawa."*

16. There are approximately 42 of Ki Padmosusastro's works kept in the Indonesia National Library. His works are also kept at the Koninkelijk Bibliotheek dan Koninkelijk Instituut voor Taal, Land en Volkenkunde in the Netherlands.

17. "Sweeping" is a uniquely Indonesian use of this word, meaning to expel.

18. James M. Rush, *Java: A Traveller's Anthology,* chapter "Eliza Ruhamah Scidmore Declares Java 'Finished; 1897," Oxford University Press, 1996.

19. *Blusukan* is a Javanese tradition of just rulers mixing with the common people to hear their concerns.

20. Agus Santosa, "The Jokowi Secrets," Gradien Mediatama, Yogyakarta, 2014.

21. Mangoendipoero, *Dancing in Stillness: The Beauty of Javanese Ethics.* The Javanese terms are *sabar, sadhiya, saleh, sareh, salaras,sembada, sumeleh, lantip, lugas, luhur, luruh, waskitha, waspadha, wibawa, widya and winasis.*

22. PewResearch Religion and Public Life Project, "Faith on the Hill: The Religious Composition of the 113th Congress," January 2, 2013

23. *Midodareni* is a traditional Javanese ceremony the night before the wedding. The groom visits the bride's family bearing gifts, waiting outside. *Midodareni* is derived from the word *Widodari* meaning goddess, the bride being as beautiful as a goddess.

24. Indonesian: *Jaga silaturahmi,* a phrase referring to importance of maintaining relationships.

25. Suwardi Endraswara, *Falsafah Hidup Jawa,* Cakrawala, 2009.

26. *Ramadan,* or *Bulan Puasa* (Fasting Month) in Indonesian, is the holy month of fasting that Muslims observe worldwide. This annual observance is regarded as one of the Five Pillars of Islam. Muslims fast from before dawn until around sunset and frequently gather with friends and relatives to break fast in a festive atmosphere. Fasting helps Muslims to be more pious and humble, conscious of the less fortunate. *Ramadan* is also a time of charity.

27. *Idul Fitri, (Eid al-fitr* in Arabic,) also called *Lebaran* in Indonesia, is a holy time marking the end of *Ramadan,* a national holiday lasting officially for two days in the Indonesian calendar. During *Lebaran,* everyone returns to their home town *(mudik)* and during the first few days of *Ramadan* take part in a special ritual called *halal bi-halal.* During this ritual, Muslim Indonesians visit their elders and show respect to them.

28. Amrozi was executed in 2008 for his act of terrorism in the 2002 Bali bombing.

29. "Global Happiness Report, ipsos-na.com, January 2014.

30. There are many words for rice in Indonesian language, depending on its state. *Nasi* is the term for cooked rice that is eaten. *Beras* is the term for uncooked rice. *Padi* is the rice growing on stalks in fields before harvest. The rice field is called *sawah.*

31. Rand Corporation, *American Public Support for U.S. Military Operations from Mogadishu to Baghdad*, 2005.

32. WorldPublicOpinion.Org, *Muslim Public Opinion on US Policy, Attacks on Civilians and al Qaeda*, (University of Maryland, April 25, 2007).

33. James Carroll, "The Bush Crusade," Truth-Out.org., September 3, 2004.

34. Azyumardi Azra, *Indonesia, Islam, and Democracy: Dynamics in a Global Context*, (Solstice Publishing, 2006); also see "The Jakarta Post," September 27, 2001.

35. America is a Sissy!" *Rakyat Merdeka*, October 7, 2001.

36. U.S. Department of State, 2001 International Religious Freedom Report.

37. Robert W. Hefner, *Global Violence and Indonesian Muslim Politics*, American Anthropologist, 2002.

38. WSWS.org, *Megawati's support for US war drive exacerbates tensions in Indonesia*, September 27, 2001.

39. See U.S. Department of State Travel Warning: Indonesia, September 24, 2001, and other travel warnings from November 2000 to May 2008.

40. Asia Wall Street Journal, Tough U.S. Envoy Ends Jakarta Stint, October 4, 2001.

41. *Rakyat Merdeka*, "Go to Hell," September 29, 2001.

42. U.S. Department of State: Country Reports on Human Rights Practices, Indonesia, 2002 (March 31, 2003).

43. Valerina Novita Daniel, *Diplomasi Public Amerika Serikat Terhadap Publik Indonesia dalam Kampanye Melawan Terorisme (Studi Kasus: Aksi Militer ke Afghanistan, 21 Sept – 22 Des 2001* (Depok 2003).

44. Pew Reseach, Global Attitudes Project, March 14, 2007.

45. Jusuf Wanandi, Member of the Board of Trustees, Center for Strategic and International Studies, Jakarta, "RI Needs to Send Clear Signals on Terrorism," *The Jakarta Post*" December 10, 2001.

46. Greg Fealy, "Is Indonesia a Terrorist Base?" *Inside Indonesia*, July-September 2003.

47. Paul Wolfowitz Interview with James Dao and Eric Schmitt, *The New York Times*, U.S. Department of Defense transcript, January 7, 2002.

48. Remarks with Indonesian Foreign Minister Hassan Wirajuda, Indonesian Ministry of Foreign Affairs transcript, August 2, 2002.

49. Abu Bakar Ba'asyir was formally the leader *Majelis Mujahidin Indonesia* (MMI) and was later convicted of giving orders to the JI terrorists to carry out terrorist attacks.

50. Italicized comments in parenthesis are author's comments.

51. Hidayatullah.com, "Ba'asyir and the Majelis Mujahidin Suspect Connection to CIA," October 14, 2002.

52. *Republika* newspaper, "The Bali Incident Is Heading in the Direction of Overseas," October 20, 2002.

53. Deputy Secretary Wolfowitz Interview with SCTV, U.S. Department of Defense transcript, November 6, 2002.

54. *Rakyat Merdeka, Kelompok Islam Tolak Dikaitkan dengan Bom Bali*, October 14, 2002.

55. *Republika, Jangan Tangkapi Tokoh Islam*, October 30, 2002.

56. Pew Research, Global Attitudes Project, March 14, 2007.

57. *Kompas, Hassan Wirajuda, Boyce, dan Irak*, December 16, 2003.

58. *Tabloid Republika, Dialog Jumat*, August 22, 2003.

59. International Crisis Group, *Indonesia: Jihadi Surprise in Aceh*, Asia Report No. 189, April 2010.

60. U.S. Department of State Archive, Charlotte Beers, Under Secretary for Public Diplomacy and Public Affairs, Remarks to the National Press Club, Washington, D.C., *Public Diplomacy After September 11*, December 18, 2002.

61. For example, see Thomas Friedman's 2002 book, *The Lexus and the Olive Tree*. Also see Fareed Zakaria, *Despite Ukraine, Mexico and Ukraine Lead Reform Efforts*, Newsmax, August 10, 2014.

62. John Esposito, Forward to book, *Islamophobia: The Challenge of Pluralism in the 21st Century*, edited by John Esposito (Oxford University Press, 2011).

63. Ibrahim Kalin, *Islamophobia and the Limits of Multiculturalism*, a chapter in the book, *Islamophobia: The Challenge of Pluralism in the 21st Century*, edited by John Esposito (Oxford University Press, 2011).

64. Pew Research Center Global Attitudes Project, July 2011: 1999/2000 survey trends provided by the Department of State.

65. Pew Research Center, October 2013.

66. PewResearch Global Attitudes Project, *Indonesia: The Obama Effect*, March 18, 2010.

67. U.S. Department of State, "United States-Indonesia Comprehensive Partnership, Office of the Spokesperson, October 8, 2013.

68. Angga Kurniawan, "*War on Terror Amerika Serikat di Indonesia: Senapan atau Bantuan.*" Pikirangga.blogspot.com, May 9, 2013.

69. Harris, Mark W., "Unitarian Origins: Our Historic Faith, Unitarian Universalist Association, 2004.

70. Spellberg, Denise A. (2013-10-01). Thomas Jefferson's Qur'an: Islam and the Founders. Knopf Doubleday Publishing Group. Kindle Edition. Of the estimated 481,000 West Africans imported into British North America as a result of the slave trade, nearly 255,000 came from areas influenced by Islam.

71 Ibid.

72. John Locke was influenced by the American Baptist theologian Roger Williams.

73. Murphy, Alex, "John Locke, Islam and the New World," Free Republic, October 13, 2010.

74. Spellberg. (2013-10-01). Thomas Jefferson's Qur'an: Islam and the Founders. Knopf Doubleday Publishing Group.

75. Ibid.

76. The First Amendment states: "Congress shall make no law respecting establishment of religion, or prohibiting the free exercise thereof..."

77. Spellberg. (2013-10-01). Thomas Jefferson's Qur'an: Islam and the Founders. Knopf Doubleday Publishing Group.

78. Muslims who are citizens of the U.S. are referred to as both American Muslims and Muslim Americans. This books refers them both ways as sources for this book used both references.

79. "Muslim Americans: Middle Class and Mostly Mainstream, PewResearchCenter, May 22, 2007.

80. Spellberg. (2013-10-01).Thomas Jefferson's Qur'an: Islam and the Founders. Knopf Doubleday Publishing Group.

81. Smith, Jane I., "Islam in America," Columbia University Press, New York, 2010.

82. Spellberg. (2013-10-01). Thomas Jefferson's Qur'an: Islam and the Founders. Knopf Doubleday Publishing Group.

83. Ibid.

84. Ibid.

85. "Being Muslim in America," U.S. Department of State, Bureau of International Information Programs, 2011.

86. Smith, Jane I., "Islam in America," Columbia University Press, New York, 2010.

87. Ibid.

88. Robert W. Hefner, *Civil Islam*, (Princeton University Press, 2000).

89. Azyumardi Azra, "Islam in Southeast Asia: Tolerance and Radicalism," paper presented at Miegunyah Public Lecture, University of Melbourne, April 6, 2005.

90. See Ahmad Syafii Maarif, chapter *Masa Depan Islam di Indonesia*, in the book *Ilusi Negara Islam*, edited by KH Abdurrahman Wahid (LibforAll 2009).

91. Ibrahim Kalin, *Islamophobia and the Limits of Multiculturalism*, a chapter in the book, *Islamophobia: The Challenge of Pluralism in the 21ˢᵗ Century*, edited by John Esposito (Oxford University Press, 2011).

92. Pew Research, Religion & Public Life Project, September 26, 2007. See also Pew Research, "How Americans Feel About Religious Groups, July 16, 2014.

93. Gallup, *Measuring the State of Muslim-West Relations: Assessing the "New Beginning"*, November 28, 2010.

94. Pew Research *Religion & Public Life Project*, April 2013.

95. Pew Research, *Religion & Public Life Project*, August 2010.

96. Pew Research *Religion & Public Life Project*, April 2013.

97. FBI 2012 Hate Crime Statistics, reported that of the 1,340 victims of an anti-religious hate crime, 62.4% were victims of an offender's anti-Jewish bias while 11.5% were victims of an anti-Islamic bias.

98. Gallup: Americans' Views of Actions in Current Middle East Conflict, July 24, 2014.

99. Jusuf Wanandi, Member of the Board of Trustees, Center for Strategic and International Studies, Jakarta, *The Jakarta Post,* "RI Needs to Send Clear Signals on Terrorism," December 10, 2001.

100. Halper, Katie, "46 examples of Muslim outrage about Paris shooting that Fox News can't seem to find," January 10, 2015, blog, "Rise Up Times."

101. Horgan, John (2014-06-16). The Psychology of Terrorism (Political Violence) (Kindle Locations 353-355). Taylor and Francis. Kindle Edition.

102. Rupert Murdoch@rupertmurdoch, Mobile.Twitter.com, January 9, 2015.

103. Henderson, Alex, "10 of the Worst Terror Attacks by Extreme Christians and Far-Right White Men," Alternet, July 24, 2013.

104. Horgan. The Psychology of Terrorism (Political Violence) (Kindle Locations 2580-2582). Taylor and Francis.

105. Armstrong, Karen (2014-10-28). Fields of Blood: Religion and the History of Violence (p. 378). Knopf Doubleday Publishing Group. Kindle Edition.

106. Ibid.

107. Ibid.

108. John L. Esposito. Who Speaks For Islam?: What a Billion Muslims Really Think (Kindle Locations 1401-1404). Kindle Edition.

109. Cesari, Jocelyne, "Islamophobia in the West: A Comparison between Europe and the United States," from Esposito, John L.; Kalin, Ibrahim (2011-03-02). Islamophobia: The Challenge of Pluralism in the 21st Century (Kindle Locations 1005-1006). Oxford University Press. Kindle Edition.

110. Francis, David, "Obama Slaps Europe for Failing to Integrate Muslims," Foreignpolicy.com, January 16, 2015.

111. Patheos Book Club. "Becoming American: A Q and A with Yvonne Haddad," September 20, 2011.

112. Esposito. Who Speaks For Islam?: What a Billion Muslims Really Think (Kindle Locations 1401-1404).

113. Ibid.

114. "Becoming American: A Q and A with Yvonne Haddad," Patheos Book Club, September 20, 2011.

115. Nurcholish Majid, *al-Quran Tentang Pluralisme dan Perdamaian*, dalam buku *Islam & Perdamaian Global*, editors Azhar Arsyad, Jawahir Thontowi, dan M. Habib Chirzin (Madyan Press Yogyakarta, 2002).

116. "One Falls, a thousand others grow" is an Indonesian expression, (*Gugur Satu, Tumbuh Seribu*) that refers to how if one person is killed in fighting for democracy and freedom, a thousand will take that person's place.

117. "Sejarah Persahabatan Korupsi Dan Birokrasi," Socio-Politica. com, July 19, 2009.

118. Stephanie Brancaforte, "A Martyr for Aceh," The Progressive, April 2001, posted on ETAN website.

119. USINDO, "Remembering Soeharto: Five Ambassadors Reflect," March 7, 2008.

120. A simple collection of small buildings and food stalls named for the street where it was located where writers, artists and political activists gathered.

121. *Komisi Untuk Orang Hilang dan Korban Tindak Kekerasan.*

122. *Lembaga Studi dan Advokasi Masyarakat.*

123. "Bali Democracy Forum is Talking About Democracy," The President Post, November 9, 2012.

124. In Indonesian, "Lapor ayam hilang, kambing pun hilang," meaning police ask for bribes to investigate crimes.

125. In Indonesian: *Datang, duduk, dengar, diam, duit.*

126. ICTJ and KontraS joint report, "Indonesia Derailed: Transitional Justice in Indonesia Since the Fall of Soeharto," March 2011.

127. Ibid.

128. ICTJ and KontraS joint report, "Indonesia Derailed: Transitional Justice in Indonesia Since the Fall of Soeharto," March 2011.

129. *Activists Dismayed by Early Release of Munir Assassin, The Jakarta Globe,* November 29, 2014.

130. Global Post, A murder trial verdict provides little closure, May 30, 2010.

131. Human Rights Watch, "Indonesia: Reopen Inquiry into Activist's Murder, February 11, 2010.

132. Gabrielson, Ryan, "Deadly Force, in Black and White," ProPublica, October 10, 2014.

133. Sabang to Merauke refers to travelling the length of Indonesia, from Sabang, Aceh in the northwest to Merauke, Papua in the southeast.

134. RapaiSaman Blogspot, "Macam-macam Tarian Aceh," April 7, 2012.

135. Yenny Rahmayati, Aceh Heritage Community Foundation, in discussing the link between culture and sustainable development at the UN Alliance of Civilization Global Forum in Bali, August 2014. Source is Endy Bayuni, The Jakarta Post, on a Facebook posting from Bali. In Acehnese: "*Matee aneuk na jeurat. Matee adat pat tamita.*"

136. Anthony Reid, *The Pre-modern Sultanate's View of its Place in the World,*" from the book, *Verandah of Violence: The Background to the Aceh Problem,* Singapore University Press, 2006.

137. Teuku Ibrahim Alfian, *Aceh and the Holy War (Prang Sabil),* from the book,*Verandah of Violence: The Background to the Aceh Problem,* Singapore University Press, 2006.

138. Anthony Reid, *Colonial Transformation: A Bitter Legacy,* from the book, *Verandah of Violence: The Background to the Aceh Problem,* Singapore University Press, 2006.

139. Adrian Morel, "Lessons from the impact evaluation of the BRA-KDP Program in Aceh," Presentation to the Development Impact Initiative, Dubai, 2010

140. Ibid.

141. Rodd McGibbon, *Local Leadership and the Aceh Conflict,* from the book, *Verandah of Violence: The Background to the Aceh Problem,* Singapore University Press, 2006.

142. Jaya Arjuna, "Ini Medan, Bung!" from the book "Medan, Bung, edited by IzHarry Agusjaya Moenzir, Tatan Daniel and Kardy Syaid, Bunga Rampai Sastra," 2010.

143. Tengku Luckman Sinar, SH, The History of Medan in the Olden Times, "Lembaga Penelitian dan Pengembangan Seni Budaya Melayu, Medan, 2005.

144. Edwin M. Loeb, Sumatra: Its History and People, Oxford University Press, 1972.

145. Fahrezi, "Demokrasi Lokal Di Sumatera Barat: Menguak Demokrasi Khas Masyarakat Minangkabau Fahrezi Blogspot, June 26, 2012.

146. Katherine Strenger Frey, Journey to the Land of the Earth Goddess, Gramedia Publishing, Jakarta, 1986.

147. Indonesian: *Seperti ayam melihat musang.*

148. Hippolito de Gama and Jao Barreto, "A Survey of Gangs and Youth Groups in Dili, Timor-Leste," A Report Prepared for AUSAID Timor-Leste, September 7, 2006.

149. "East Timor Revisited: Ford, Kissinger and the Indonesian Invasion, 1975-76, The National Security Archive, December 6, 2001.

150. Ibid.

151. ETAN, "The Santa Cruz Massacre, November 12, 1991," November 11, 2013.

152. ICTJ and KontraS joint report, "Indonesia Derailed: Transitional Justice in Indonesia Since the Fall of Soeharto," March 2011.

153. Elsam, Betty Yolanda, "Placing the Final Report of the Commission of Truth and Friendship Indonesia – Timor-Leste in the Process of the Settlement of Past Human Rights Violations in Indonesia: A Critical Evaluation," July 2010.

154. War Crimes Studies Center, University of California Berkeley, The Commission on Truth and Friendship Overview, 2014.

INDEX

DEMOS 161
Detik.com 98
Didu, M. Said 73
Dili 217, 219, 234
di Tiro, Hasan 189, 195
Divine Science 114, 226
dog 58
durian 4, 62, 63, 204, 225
Dutch 6, 7, 22, 70, 114, 166, 187, 188, 189, 200, 201, 215
Dutch New Guinea 215

E

earthquake in West Sumatra, 2009 207
East Timor 171, 217, 218, 219, 220, 221, 235
East Timor referendum 220
Egypt xvi, 70
elderly 54
Eluay, Theys 214
Emmerson, Don 104
e pluribus unum xvi
Esposito, John 104, 108, 135, 229, 231, 232
evacuation of U.S. Embassy Jakarta 92

F

family xi, xiii, xxii, 4, 5, 7, 9, 13, 18, 19, 32, 34, 39, 41, 42, 43, 44, 47, 48, 49, 50, 51, 52, 53, 59, 63, 91, 92, 95, 98, 105, 118, 122, 150, 153, 156, 165, 168, 191, 201, 225, 226, 227
FBI 72, 139, 231
Ferguson, Missouri 174
First Amendment of the

Constitution 116
Flight 93 68
Ford, Gerald 219
Forum for Harmony Among Religions in Medan 144
Fox News 131, 132, 232
Free Aceh 185
Free Aceh Movement (GAM) 185, 189, 191, 192, 193, 194, 195, 196
Free Papua 214
Fretilin 219
Friedman, Thomas 105, 229
Fuadi, Ahmad 145
Fulbright Scholarship Program 104

G

Garuda Airlines 171, 172
Gates, Bill 32
Gayo 187, 194
Gayo highlands 194
Gelbard, Robert 77
Golkar 74, 153
Goodyear rubber plantation, North Sumatra 202
Gore, Al 34
Griffiths, Mike 203
Gunungkidul 58
Gurdwara Sahib temple in Medan 200
Gus Dur 12, 120, 145, 159, 162. *See also* Wahid, Abdurrahman
Gusman, Irman 211

H

Habibie, B.J. 154, 161
Habitat for Humanity 98
Haddad, Yvonne 136, 232

Hamas 128
Hamzah, Jafar Siddiq 152
happiness x, 59
Harsha, Annisa Genevieve 45, 57
Harsha, Genevieve 113
Harsha, James 113, 139
Harsha, Sean Ralph iv, 46
Hartono, Eric 68
hate crimes 72, 128, 174
Hatta, Mohammad 7
Hawaii 33, 68
Haz, Hamzah 75
Hefner, Robert 104, 120
Helsinki Peace Agreement of 2005 191
Hendropriyono, Abdullah M. 89
Herodotus 204
Hinduism 113
hip hop 106
Hispanic Americans 174
Holland 17, 188
Horgan, John 232
human bondage 167
human rights x, xxiii, 17, 71, 120, 152, 153, 160, 161, 162, 163, 167, 169, 170, 171, 172, 173, 174, 196, 197, 210, 220, 221, 223
Human Rights Commission (Komnas HAM) 161, 170, 220
Human Rights Watch Coordinating Group (HRWG) 161
human slavery 115, 160
Hume, Cameron 25, 27, 111, 163
Huntington, Samuel 163
Hussein, Saddam 96

I

Idul Fitri ix, x, xi, 45, 51, 52, 57, 164, 178, 227
India xvi, 34, 117, 173, 187, 188, 191, 199, 200, 201
Indian 173, 187, 188, 191, 199, 200
Indonesia Church Forum (FGI) 144
Indonesian Army (TNI) 192, 193, 194, 221
Indonesian Association of Families of the Disappeared (IKOHI) 170
Indonesian Democratic Party (PDI) 153, 156
Indonesian Foreign Ministry 178
Indonesian Heritage Trust in Medan 200
Indonesian National Police 72
Institute for Policy Research and Policy (Elsam) 160, 235
Institute for the Free Flow of Information (ISAI) 159
International Monetary Fund (IMF) 156
International Organization for Migration (IOM) 178
International Visitor Leadership Program 104
Iran 71
Iraq xvii, 21, 71, 82, 85, 96, 107, 109, 110, 133, 134, 135, 176, 178, 224
Irian Jaya 214
Irwandi, Yusuf 192
Iskandar Muda 187

Kurdistan, Iraq 178

L

Lake Toba, North Sumatra 204
Lampung 152, 212
Langsa, Aceh 193
Lani 209
Lapangan Merdeka in Medan 201
Laskar Jihad (Warriors of Jihad) 71, 74
Legal Aid Foundation 152
Leuser 194, 202, 203
Lhokseumawe, Aceh 184
liberal 33, 114, 115, 119, 123, 124, 128, 134, 222
Libya xvi, 71
Liddle, Bill 104
Lieberman, Joe 34
Locke, John 116, 230
London Sumatra building in Medan 201
Lubis, Fadhil 45, 142
Lubis, Mochtar 140

M

Maarif, Syafii 71, 75, 94, 104, 120, 121, 231
Madison, James 115
Madjid, Nurcholish 104, 120, 143
Madoff, Bernie 33
Mahmudin, Ali 35
Maimun Palace in Medan 200
Majapahit Empire 6, 225
Malaysia 14, 87, 117, 119, 156, 176, 177, 179
Malcolm X 114
Maluku Islands 170

Manado 176
Manaf, Muzakir 195
Mangoendipoero, Henny 8
Mangoendipoero, Noeke Ratna Padmiandari xxiv, 6, 9, 10, 29, 57, 225
Mangoendipoero, Padmosawego 8, 9, 40, 42, 57
Mangoendipoero, Siti Soendari 9, 57
Medan xv, 44, 45, 63, 99, 100, 106, 142, 144, 152, 153, 184, 189, 193, 199, 200, 201, 202, 203, 205, 234
Media Indonesia, newspaper 83
Merauke xii, 180, 181, 233
Meulaboh 193
Mexican-Americans 49
Migrant Care 178
migrant workers terminal, Soekarno Hatta Airport 177
Minang 187, 199, 200, 206, 209, 210, 211, 234
Minangkabau 187, 199, 210, 211, 234
Mobil Oil 184
Moerdani, Benny 154
Mohamad, Goenawan 158
Morris, Greta 79
Mount Leuser National Park 202, 203
Muhammadiyah xviii, 71, 75, 80, 94, 107, 120, 142, 159, 206
Mujahadeen 71
Mujahidin 94, 229
Mulyani, Sri 36
Munawar, Said Agil 75

Philippines 87
pig 58, 205
politeness 10, 56
Polo, Marco 204
Portuguese 188, 200, 218
Powell, Colin 137
Priyanto, Pollycarpus 172
Prosperous Justice Party (PKS)
  81, 94
Protestants 34, 114, 115, 116
Puritan 114
Purowadi 35

Q

Qanun Jinayat 196

R

racism in America 33
Rais, Amien 104, 120, 159
Rakyat Merdeka, newspaper
  72, 74, 83, 87, 91, 159,
  228, 229
Ramadan ix, x, xii, 51, 106,
  227
Ramage, Doug 104
Ranggawarsito 17
Rangsang Tuban 17
Rawamangun 3, 5, 41
reformasi 120, 160, 161, 173,
  215
religious freedom 106, 113,
  114, 116
religious tolerance xxiii, 83,
  119, 223
Remarkable Current 106
rencong xii, 183, 188
Republicans 123
Republika, newspaper 83, 85,
  86, 87, 88, 94, 98, 99,
  229
Reverend Lase 205

Ritz-Carlton Hotel Jakarta 97

S

Sabah, Aceh 196
Sabang xii, 180, 181, 233
Sabili magazine 83, 84
Sageman, Marc 134
Salem, Massachusetts 114
Salman, Ubay 84
same sex marriage 53
Samosir Island, North Sumatra
  204
Sand Creek Massacre of 1864
  173
Santa Cruz massacre of 1991
  220, 235
Sanur 43
Saptohoedojo 38
Sardono 19
Satan 68, 158
Saudi Arabia 70, 176, 177
Scidmore, Eliza Ruhamah 21,
  226
SCTV 93, 229
Seceders 113
security forces 70, 99, 169,
  170, 171, 218, 220, 221
September 11, 2001 xxiii, 21,
  67, 68, 76
September 30, 1965 70
"Shared Values" campaign
  105
sharia law 126, 196, 197
Shi'ism 118
Siam 188
Sigli, Aceh 193
Sikhs 72
Sinabung volcano, North
  Sumatra 205
Sinar Harapan, newspaper
  151
Sinar, Tengku Luckman 200

About the Author

STANLEY HARSHA came to Indonesia in 1986 on his first overseas assignment as a United States diplomat. Like most people who set foot in Indonesia, he fell in love with the people and culture. He had four assignments in Indonesia, spanning 12 years of his 28-year career with the U.S. Department of State. He most recently served as U.S. Consul for Sumatra (2009-2011), with previous assignments as Deputy Political Counselor (2007-2009), Press Attaché (2001-2004) and Public Affairs Officer for Sumatra (1987-1990). During these years he dealt with many issues, from religious tolerance and terrorism to democracy building and human rights, as well as with earthquakes and volcanic eruptions.

He also served as Charge d'affaires, a.i. in Timor-Leste in 2007, and has been posted to Beijing, Kuala Lumpur, Taiwan, and Namibia. In Washington, D.C., he most recently was a Senior Advisor for the Bureau of Educational and Cultural Affairs at the U.S. State Department (2012-2013) and as Executive Director of the Fulbright Foreign Scholarship Board (2011-2012).

Since retiring as a diplomat in 2013, Stanley has divided his time between his homes in Conifer, Colorado and Indonesia. He now dedicates himself to writing, building bilateral education ties, and promoting religious tolerance.

His wife, Henny, is from Solo, Central Java, and they have two grown children.

Before becoming a diplomat, Stanley was a journalist in the U.S. and in Venezuela. He graduated from the University of Colorado in Boulder, and also studied at Universidad de Costa Rica and Universidad de Mexico. He is fluent in Indonesian, Malaysian, Spanish and Mandarin Chinese.

Made in the USA
San Bernardino, CA
19 May 2016